Praise for *Speak It Plain*

"*Authentic* and *genuine* are words I use to describe the blessings that Meta Carlson has gifted us with through her writing. There's truth and honesty spoken in these blessings and liturgies that point to Whose we are and feed our hungry spirits for today."
—**Rev. Karen Stevensen**, LICSW

"*Speak it Plain* invites us into the life of God and the lives of God's people. These blessings, prayers, and rituals are for our real and shared human experience. Meta Carlson's words plant us in the soil on which we already stand, bidding us to grow deep and to reach wide."
—**Jeni Grangaard**, Luther Seminary Pastor

"*Speak It Plain* is a gift to Christian leaders who want to create, grow, and nurture more inclusive and welcoming congregations. You will find compassionate blessings and poems for those who come to our faith communities, new understandings of the liturgical service, and more. Meta Carlson, a gifted parish pastor, offers insights and tools to Christian leaders to better connect the teachings of the church to how we live our lives today!"
—**Diane Waarvik**, Director of Congregational Care, Bethlehem Lutheran Church, Twin Cities

"There are no perfect words, for they are as ordinary and broken as the vessels that carry them. Yet in *Speak It Plain*, Meta Carlson reminds us with her reclamation that the cosmic mystery of our gracious God meets us precisely here—in plain words. Truly, Meta is the wordsmith the church has been waiting for, offering elegantly earthy ways to speak the living Word anew among the worshiping body of Christ."
—**Justin Lind-Ayres**, pastor and author of *Is That Poop on My Arm? Parenting While Christian*

"For such a time as this, *Speak It Plain* has come to us to remind, reveal, and reaffirm all the areas of our life in need of God's great and gentle love. It is an invitation to steep ourselves in this love. This is exactly the book I am looking for when I'm invited to share a devotion or wanting to share a word of hope with a friend, colleague, or family member when words escape me. Meta Carlson has a divine gift and a honed talent that translates to the heart."

—**Kris Bjorke (she, her, hers)**, Service Learning Project Manager, 2021 ELCA Youth Gathering

"With words both revelatory and full of remembering, Meta Carlson gives us a lively collection of promising paths toward a deeper understanding of how we might do church in a rapidly changing world. Her plain-spoken, transparent style allows empathic, hopeful insights to shine easily through."

—**John Hermanson**, liturgist, musician

Speak It Plain

*Words for Worship
and Life Together*

Meta Herrick Carlson

Fortress Press
Minneapolis

SPEAK IT PLAIN
Words for Worship and Life Together

Copyright © 2020 Meta Herrick Carlson. Published by Fortress Press, an imprint of 1517 Media. All rights reserved. Except for brief quotations in critical articles or reviews, no part of this book may be reproduced in any manner without prior written permission from the publisher. Email copyright@1517.media or write to Permissions, Fortress Press, PO Box 1209, Minneapolis, MN 55440-1209.

Purchase of this book comes with permission to reproduce portions intended for group use. To access this reproducible material, see page 196.

Print ISBN: 978-1-5064-5063-6
eBook ISBN: 978-1-5064-5064-3

Cover artwork: Nature Art © Bernardo Ramonfaur | Dreamstime.com
Cover design: Laurie Ingram
Interior design and typesetting: PerfecType, Nashville, TN

For Christian public leaders telling truth to power
For parish pastors serving with love and healthy boundaries
For the questions people are actually asking
For the church, which is always dying and rising

Contents

PREFACE xi

SECTION I
POEMS, PRAYERS, AND SEASONAL BLESSINGS

1 Blessing Poems and Prayers 3

   For People: Anxious Ones, Busy Adults, Caregivers, Children, Church Musicians, Church Staff, Deacons, Elders, Families Forming, Families Waiting, Forgotten Ones, Godparents, Graduates, Immigrants, Pastors, Peacemakers, Prisoners, Protesters, Refugees, Snowbirds, Students, Those Who Haven't Been to Church Yet, Those Who Left, Victims of Violence, Volunteers, Weary Ones, Worship Leaders, Young Adults

   For Relationships: Celebrating the LGBTQIA+ Community, Church and Politics, Climate Care, Consent Culture, Ecumenical Relations, Interfaith Connections, Stolen Land

   For Moments: Accompaniment, After a Mass Shooting, A New Year, Anointing Another, Community Organizing,

Courage, Family before the Funeral, Gathering as a Semblance, Going to Camp, Healthy Boundaries, Home Communion, Hospice Care, Infertility, Leaders Feeling Stuck, Loss, Making Medical Decisions, Money Talk, Moving into the Unknown, Planting a Garden, Planting a Memorial Tree, Political or Civic Grief, Pregnancy or Infant Loss, Sending a Group, Taking a Sabbatical, Veterans, Waiting Together, Welcoming Guests on Holidays

2 For the Seasons 59

    Advent 60

    Saint Lucia Day 61

    Blue Christmas 62

    Day of Epiphany 64

    Baptism of Our Lord 65

    Transfiguration Day 66

    Ash Wednesday 67

    Holy Saturday 68

    The Easter Season 69

    Ascension Day 71

    Pentecost 72

    Holy Trinity Sunday 73

    (Extra) Ordinary Time 74

    Reformation Day 75

    All Saints' Day 76

    Christ the King 78

CONTENTS

SECTION II
Liturgies, Litanies, and Special Services

3 The Church Confesses 83
    The Church Confesses: For Sexual Shame 85
    The Church Confesses: For White Supremacy 87
    The Church Confesses: For Self-Preservation 91

4 Celebrating Baptism 95
    Thanksgiving for Baptism 96
    Baptizing a Child 98
    Baptizing an Adult 104
    Affirmation of Baptism and Naming Ceremony 112
    Affirmation of Baptism or Confirmation of Faith 114
    A Blessing for the Baptized 121
    A Swift or Private Baptism 122

5 Teaching Liturgy in Worship 125
    Celebrating First Communion 126
    Teaching the Lord's Prayer 129
    Children Receiving Study Bibles 131
    Teaching the Nicene Creed 134
    Blessing Students Beginning Confirmation 137

6 Litanies for Worship 143
    Farewell to a Lay Staff Member 144
    Farewell to a Pastor or Deacon 146
    For a Congregation Closing 148

CONTENTS

    For a New Congregation 150

    For New Members. 151

    For Clergy Misconduct 153

    For Congregational Grief and Trauma 154

    For Congregations Coming Together. 156

    For Installing Lay Leaders 157

    For Interim Leaders. 159

    For Installing a Pastor or Deacon. 160

7 Special Services 163

    For Blessing a Neighborhood. 169

    For Healing and Wholeness. 173

    For Recovery and Mental Health 177

    For Separation or Divorce 181

    For Celebration of Marriage 183

    For a Memorial Service 188

    For a Graveside Committal 191

Acknowledgments 195

About the Author 197

Preface

I have been writing poems and rituals since I was a teenager, so when I became a parish pastor, I started to mess with liturgy, too. My childhood in the church was shaped by words and melodies that rarely changed, that welcomed me each Sunday morning and found a way into the core of my memory. My family moved a few times while I was growing up, so I spent several years navigating new places and feeling unfamiliar. The comfort and repetition of liturgy was tucked into these layers of early life, a constant conversation invited by the same worn hymnals no matter where we called home.

But liturgy makes a lot of assumptions about the people gathered for worship and the spiritual conversation we are craving. For five hundred years, my Christian tradition has been asking Martin Luther's favorite question: *What does this mean?* Our liturgy takes a scholarly approach to this curiosity each week, but I'm not sure that cuts to the heart of the hunger and wonder you'll find at Sunday brunch, soccer practice, or worship these days.

Since the Bible is no longer the dominant narrative in America, worship leaders cannot assume people know the stories, experience God a particular way, or feel familiar with the language we've been using for generations. This book invites leaders to consider how great theology is hiding beneath our high church language, our patriarchal customs, and our insular questions.

This resource includes opportunities for corporate confession on behalf of the church, language that models healthy boundaries, and words for marking life events such as separation or divorce, political or civic grief, and anointing people in transition. *Speak It Plain* is a companion to the resources you already use for planning worship and living together in Christian community.

My prayer is that these words will help you speak it plain, that the weight of unspoken trauma will lose its power, that the work of the people will be reclaimed by the people, and that the assembly will be inspired to create deeper connections between worship and the questions we're asking today.

Section I

Poems, Prayers, and Seasonal Blessings

1

Blessing Poems and Prayers

My three small children attend worship most Sundays with my spouse. Most of my glances in their direction suggest they aren't paying much attention. There's a lot of snacking, poking, coloring, and wiggling in that pew. But then, driving home, I'm proven wrong.

Why do you put oil on people's foreheads?
If Jesus had brown skin, why does he have white skin in my Bible?
Where is Yemen?
Why do we all shake hands in the middle of worship?
I saw a lady crying, and another lady moved over to hold her hand.

Their senses are engaged. Children are paying attention to what gets airtime in worship, what feelings we normalize, who matters, and what kind of language we use to talk about God's unconditional love and our human suffering.

As a preacher, I care deeply about what people see and hear during worship. I want my kids to grow up knowing their church has something to say about the systems that further oppress those who are already crushed by the empire. I want them to learn to talk about the stewardship of resources, serving the poor, and building community like Jesus did. If it mattered to Jesus, it should matter to the words we speak aloud in worship.

This section is filled with poems for worship and devotional use. It reminds me of the pile on my desk that cannot be filed away properly, because the contents are too miscellaneous, too contextual and urgent to hide. Like the pile, this section kept growing during the writing process.

There are always more reasons to bless people, more relationships to honor, and more moments to ordain, but I had to stop so this book could be born. I hope these pieces inspire you to write blessings that your community needs in order to live and be free in Christ.

For People

Anxious Ones

There is stealthy restoration in singing together,
for it pulls our panicked breathing into one chorus
of wind between measures, drawing deeply
from where we need not be frightened.

Our bodies are fearfully and wonderfully made,
with chemicals and instincts to protect
who we are and what we already have.
But this is mere survival, a barely being place.

How risky, then, that God is calling us
out of our shallow gasps for air
and into the deep, abundant breath of life,
robust melodies that move us forward.

It is difficult to feel this wind all alone,
so remember to sing together and often,
always expanding the body and making room
for shalom and the Spirit in the heart of your song.

Busy Adults

Remember the Sabbath.
It is not a suggestion, but rather
the first of all commands, for God knew
we would need this rhythm of rest
in the beginning and every generation since.

Even and especially in the middle of life,
when we are called by so many names
that belong to duty and performance,
that call us away from our first and forever name:
Beloved Child of God.

You are surrounded by generations
and expectations that will never tire
of asking more from you,
filling your days with obligation
that is both rich and weary,
that tempts you to forget you are mortal.

God, grant us the courage to rest,
to resist the idols of busy and best,
to learn to stand ourselves long enough
to hear you call our name, to notice what
you are making, even without our help and hindrance.

Bless our deep breaths, our long sighs,
and our fearful fidgets so that we trust your presence
in our nothingness and learn to believe
the world will keep spinning and
it is enough to simply be your people.

Caregivers

Your work is incarnate,
received by the flesh of another.
A portion of yourself handed over,
often without question or answer.

It is both holy and mundane,
this watching and waiting,
these routines and rhythms
a meter for your hours and days.

Lest you disappear into this service,
hear these words of blessing for your body:

How you are showing up matters.
What you are doing and giving matters.
You are seen and loved in the midst
of this labor on behalf of another.

When you have been poured out,
may the Spirit grant rest that fuels
your health, your strength, your joy,
and other sense of purpose,
so that you receive good care
and a fresh anointing for what still lies ahead.

Children

May you find a joyful welcome
at the heart of this assembly,
so these adults never forget
they were once children themselves.

May your eyes and ears gather good stories
about what really matters to God,
so that love has the loudest word
whenever the world tries to say otherwise.

May your whole sense of self know safety here,
honored and loved beyond measure
according to the promises
we spoke over you in baptism and ever since.

May your life know value and purpose,
for you have been called and set free
to be hope and justice for those who do not know
they are already and always enough.

May you go boldly into the world,
but find your way home whenever
you need these sights and sounds
that know who and whose you are.

Church Musicians

You are conducting a conversation
with song and instrumentation,
writing Scripture on our hearts
with music even dementia remembers.

We'd like to think these sounds are inspired
by the choirs of angels in heaven,
the saints before and after us, and
the music that has always been in our souls
just waiting to come alive in community.

But you guide our breath into one
and teach us to let it out beautifully and together.
Bless each pitch you give us,
the long introductions while we find the right page,
the quiet mastery and late-night rehearsals.
Your melodic sermons are a sweet marriage between
the church that has been and the one we are still becoming.

Church Staff

Blessed are you who work
in the shadow of the steeple
for the sake of those
who are not yet here
and those who know nothing else,
where faithful mission can be swallowed
by the business of the church.

You have seen the gospel
tamed by our fear of what's next,
but you also know the holy power
of many becoming together.

Blessed are you who work
strange hours for the sake of
those who gather,
longing to be known by the One
we mention so casually.
Your quiet task is focused
on the details of each tree
so that others may come and
admire the whole forest at once.

Blessed are you who build trust
where trust has been broken.

Blessed are you who are honest
about what has been hidden.

Blessed are you who do justice
where sin has shattered peace.

Blessed are you who bear love
where people seek grace.

Your labor is not in vain and
your faith bears Christ to
all who come weary.

Deacons

The call is to stand between,
in the liminal and fuzzy boundaries
where church and world blur,
coaxing folks out of stark categories
and into real life where proclaiming the gospel
and serving the neighbor are never separate.

You are ordained for action
that embodies God's love on the margins
and moves people toward purpose and love
that do not require a crucifix, font, or altar.

Instead you show them how God lived in a body,
wrapping a towel at your waist,
stooping down to fill a basin with water,
washing and drying your neighbor's feet
with such care, they are certain
they've seen Jesus.

Elders

May the confessions and grief
be released now, and with honesty
that does not waste dignity or time.
We are still waiting on the wisdom you share.

May you seek your legacy
in relationships and love that live
long after structures crumble
and social norms fade.

May you be inspired
by your descendants now rising,
inviting their spirituality and questions
into the heart of the conversation.

May you be brave in this season,
letting go and holding on, believing
at the direction of the Holy Spirit that
we are not nearly finished dying and rising.

Families Forming

Your love is courage that opens itself
to the possibility of one another,
forming family and making promises
while systems and paperwork run to catch up.

Your love is honest about the wilderness
of becoming and belonging
without knowing much of anything for certain,
only that you are willing to try with your whole heart.

Your love is strengthened by God's Spirit,
who already knows we are meant for each other,
where sacred kinship waits and declares
we are safe and valuable and home.

Families Waiting

There are still too many things lying in wait
like loose threads to unravel your tender plans.
After dark, you stare at the ceiling and wonder
whether all the other families have kissed goodnight.

There is worry in the waiting,
and what could be is so very thin.
This is how the waiting begs to be shared,
to be brokered by those who love you
as one body, bearing the unknown together.
We will come and wait with you until you decide
it does not feel like waiting anymore.

Forgotten Ones

The church has not always remembered
to love you with wild abandon,
to go looking for you in far pasture,
to delight in the good fortune of being near you.

But Jesus welcomed interruptions and strangers
as opportunities for love handed over
like portals that reveal how fiercely
you deserve to be known and remembered.

So when the church draws boundaries
around people and power that leave you outside,
remember that the only lines Jesus drew
set him on the side of the forgotten and oppressed.

You are standing on holy ground,
in the presence of the God who cannot forget you,
who sees and hears you, who comes near you.
May the church learn to do likewise.

Godparents

Stop to notice
the details of the big day:
Are there birds singing, and
who is the oldest saint
in the pews while promises bellow?

Watch the faces of this family
while they bring a child
to death and love and life,
a mystery swirling
in the waters of baptism.

Light the candle
and marry your promise to God's,
that you will help this one shine
brightly so the world sees
who they actually are: Beloved.

These details become the story
you will tell hundreds of times
about the day their cosmic value
took root in human history, with truth
that was sweet like cake and song.

Graduates

You have been shaped by the requirements
of progress and adolescent freedom,
but these statistics and awards are
not all of who you are. Not even close.

Whether you know it or not,
whether you like it or not,
we are helping God keep the promises that extend
beyond what you can do and earn in this world.

We remember your first and forever name:
Beloved Child of God. No matter how far
you wander in any direction,
we will remember what is already and always true.

You are already and always enough.
You are fearfully and wonderfully made.
You are more than one thing to God and to us.
So graduate from some things, but not everything.
Not this.

Immigrants

Our Scripture declares
the power of newcomers
over and over again, calling
their grit and wisdom

necessary
holy
gift
revelation.

You are breath and life
for a country still being born,
still learning to confess and love and share,
still dreaming of a more perfect union.

Blessed are the immigrants,
for you have traveled in the hand of God
like our storied saints and ancestors

Abraham
Joseph
Moses
Ruth
Daniel
Jesus.

Turn your face toward belonging here.
You are a gift of the Spirit.
You are a generous sign that this nation is
not nearly finished being beautiful.

Pastors

There is a holy tension in this call
to be set apart but not above,
making promises that strain your faith
and get bent by the fullness of people
you are ordained to love uniquely.

They are looking for Jesus, and instead
they get you, an ordinary person
with sacred, restless nerve that manifests
a thousand different ways over time.

Just remember that you are not called
to make them happy or to save the church,
but to preach the good news
and administer the sacraments.

Lives are moved by the real presence of Jesus
who is still here, who cares more about
changing the church than saving it, too.

Peacemakers

This blessing has come near to your work
and has already noticed a rumble beneath our feet.
This feels different from preservation,
for making begins beyond the instinct to protect
and the hesitation around loss.

Your making will not settle for what has already been
and pushes on possibility without waiting for permission.
It is powerful and free, which threatens the veneer
of circumstances long unchallenged.
They will tell you to quiet down or stop altogether.

Persist, you maker of peace, in defiance of every invitation
to use your power for something else. Showing up matters
and, like the earth's tremble, can leave cracks in the façades
that need to fall away in favor of peace stirred up for all.

Prisoners

Blessed are you who pay with your time,
trapped inside the system and outside community.
Have you heard about the God who comes down
to free the captives, to release the prisoners,
to be in the suffering, so it can be known
and then broken by heaven's love?

Woe to those who harbor hate,
who put you out of sight and mind,
and decide about your life and value,
fixing their eyes on Jesus
and yet unwilling to see.

You are God's own beloved,
worthy of new life and every human dignity.
And so we wait with you, in love and prayer,
until we are reconciled and liberated as one people.
And we work with you, for equal justice under the law,
until all people are safe and whole.

Protesters

There will always be good reasons
to stand in the face of empire,
to speak truth to power,
to take blows on behalf of the meek,
to come alongside the lonely and least.

The kingdom of heaven has yet to find
an earthly governance or ruler
worthy of our praise and eager trust.
without a deep need for resistance,
prophets to speak both warning and promise.

The front lines do not know
instant gratification or perfect change,
but a call to fierce and holy tension
between what is and what could still be.
So step forward and receive a fresh anointing
for the work that is never finished.

Refugees

Your plight is tangled up
with our whole human story.
We have been drawing lines
and fleeing since the dawn of time.

Blessed are you, mothers
who nurse your babies with hope
even after your milk has dried.

Blessed are you, young men,
who are wise with good reasons
you cannot return home safely.

Blessed are you, the able-bodied,
who pace the caravan with grace and
wait for the weary ones to catch up.

Blessed are you, who leave everything,
who do not or cannot look back again
in your pursuit of peace and new life.

Blessed are you, broken in body and spirit,
fractured by terror, illness, and famine,
struck down but not destroyed.

Blessed are you who wait and come,
you are resurrection and life in the flesh,
you are a new vision of peace on earth.

Snowbirds

In case we don't tell you
often enough, we watch
for your going out and coming in.

There is a mark in the sky
holding space between us,
like a jet-stream cord
that does not fade
once you are out of sight.

It gathers us gently
across the months and miles
stretching church farther than
we'd think to do
if you'd stayed right here all along.

Godspeed.
And welcome home.
Both are gift and delight.

Students

The world has enough people
who have stopped learning,
who have already decided,
who have fixed their minds
on a few possibilities.

So thank God for your learning,
your creative curiosity still stirring!
Your questions make a holy mess
of mundane assumptions
and the status quo's attitude.

The Spirit is at work in every new thing—
the discoveries and challenges of
a more complex and interesting world.
God delights in what you seek and find,
for this is creation still becoming new.

Those Who Haven't Been to Church Yet

This blessing seeks to find you
who have not been to church yet,
you who do not know that
a community already loves you.

Their prayers are holding wide space
for who you are and what you need
so that if you decide to come, you will see
that they are not finished becoming.

They are a mess of a people who are
more curious than certain about most things.
But they gather for the sake of connection,
and a faith that's too heavy to carry all alone.

They sent this blessing so you would know.
Even if you never come at all,
you are loved already and always.

Those Who Left

We still speak your name fondly,
each time recalling how much
you mattered here.

Our memories are filled
with gratitude, but also regret
that pulls us into the past.

It hurt to watch you,
our loved one, leave,
because we were one body.
And we are one body still.

We are missing you and also,
we offer a blessing for your exodus,
trusting the Spirit we still share
to hold us together
in the cosmic order of things unseen,
while also pulling us forward into tomorrow.

Victims of Violence

Has anyone listened to the words you can muster,
or waded in your silent currents of despair and rage?
Someone is standing in the midst of your suffering,
feeling all that cannot be explained or released.

Jesus has called us to love like this,
to stand in the suffering and bear witness
to the ways you are being torn apart
from safety and your priceless value.

The church still is learning to love like this,
to stand alongside without pretense or defense,
to honor your body, mind, and spirit as beloved
with a sacrifice for what is justice and merciful.

The church still is learning to be vulnerable,
to live like communal suffering relieves pain
and reveals the power of Christ crucified,
but we are still so afraid. Lord, have mercy.

Still, someone is surely standing beside you,
listening and believing, holding and weeping,
dying and rising without hesitation, because
you always have been worthy of tending and witness.

Volunteers

It is not only what you do,
but how you connect and love
that can transform a role or task
into a gift from God.

God bless your showing up
and the details of your doing.

God bless your willingness
to fail and learn from the process.

God bless your humility and humor
in the heart of what you do best.

God bless your duty and joy
for this community and impact.

God bless your candor
about what really matters to you.

God bless your flexibility
about the details and outcome alike.

God bless your observations
about who else might be invited to help.

God bless your stepping back
so another can participate more fully.

God bless your openness
to a process of becoming together.

For these are the gifts of God.
And so are you.

Weary Ones

We have glorified and glamorized
the language of fighting as faithfulness,
but do not forget that there is also
beauty and faithfulness in surrender.

Lay your head down and trust that
God's strength is found here,
in your simple posture and tired soul.
Return to your mortality and breathe.

You are allowed to feel emptied
in the midst of more to do,
even in the midst of those who never tire.
Your weariness is a worthy offering.

Did you miss the good news?
Your weariness is a worthy offering!

May the cause inspire your comrades
to honor the primal need and quiet desire for rest,
and to call others to action on your behalf,
for in this body we carry each other.

Worship Leaders

In the midst of tending details,
filling schedules, and confirming tasks,
you find familiar patterns.
There is some comfort and purpose,
whether you prefer a quiet rhythm
behind the scenes or an amplified place
out front.

But these roles are not domestic
in the house of an untamed God,
where mystery rises like incense,
like words to challenge our spirit and song,
like people changed by morsels and sips,
like a red flame that burns brightly
even after we scatter
like grain without silos.

You tend a wild and holy place,
not to temper or polish too smooth,
but to witness with wonder
these textures and layers of faith.
God is weaving welcome

through who you have been
and who you are still becoming together.

So hold gently all that remains unfinished
and bless the jagged edges,
for it is here on the seams
you find connection and strength
that can make this assembly brand new.

Young Adults

Stepping out from the familiar
pattern and texture of one's youth
does not happen all at once,
or with a sure sequence,
no matter how eager or planned.

It is a sensational rush,
the delightful stimulus and terrifying silence
that surrounds you while
more of yourself is uncovered
for the world to behold.

Parts of you are still forming,
so these have become gorgeous seasons
for incarnate living,
for testing the fullness of your heart and body
before your mind gets made up.

God cries for these wild and holy years
to be unleashed for the sake of the world,
for there is good and sacred magic
in your curious exploration,
an antidote for this disenchanted age.

May the questions you ask
and the possibilities you find
be bread for your life's journey
and a gift to those who need to be reminded
of the power that comes from being uncovered.

For Relationships

Celebrating the LGBTQIA+ Community

It has been said that "All are welcome"
means the gates are wide for wolves and sheep
to enter in, defeating the purpose of the gate.
If it is not safe for sheep, then you may find only wolves.

Blessed are you, who name the codes and platitudes
the church uses to comfort the comfortable.
You who have been welcomed, but as portions of yourself,
as fragments of a person, into limitations of sacred love.

Blessed are you, who challenge simple binaries
with good theology and the image of God.
Your courage and faith magnify the Creator's delight
for our true and unique selves, a gift to the church and the world.

Church and Politics

We have funded wars and colonized nations,
stripping land and whole cultures away,
condoned slavery for votes and economy,
so don't tell me we are not political.

The gospel is good news for the people,
but so often the church has stood between
the people and their good news,
claiming hands tied or minutiae too complex.

The empire wars from age to age,
beckons the church to sell out
for the price of a gilded cage and a bullhorn,
so we can still sing and sound like we're free.

Meanwhile, the people wait for good news
from heaven, for their patience has worn thin
listening to our promises to turn the world
upside down with love and belonging from heaven.

Jesus broke bread and body
so there would be scrappy edges,
so we could see the sharp and gory danger
of this news, so we could taste and be satisfied

with plenty still to offer the world, passing baskets
until all are fed and free.
It is political, because it is for the people, the same ones
we ignore when we say it is not our place to get political.

Climate Care

This blessing aches for the gifts of creation
squandered by human dominion and the space we have put
between ourselves and the whole of creation
as though we are separate consumers.

This blessing winces at the ways God's people
abdicate responsibility for creation's care,
the most ancient of commandments,
to economic and partisan priorities.

This blessing is looking for language to tell the cosmos
that we take the creative world for granted,
resourcing the sources of all life and peace
without reverence for God and our grandchildren.

Creative world, draw us out of ourselves and renew our love for
    you,
so that we would see with new eyes the generations of making,
so that we would learn to be tender and generous,
so that we would feel deeply our connections in this life
and our Maker, who desires this sacrifice
rather than the whole earth as a burnt offering.

Consent Culture

When Jesus notices and heals people,
it begins with observation,
compassion, a coming alongside
with deep peace that knows
who they are and what they need.
May the church become a place
where people receive holy attention!

Blessed are you who need space,
who desire patience and communication,
who wish to build consent and trust.

And blessed are you who are comfortable,
who assume you are familiar enough,
but are learning what others need to feel safe.

There is no right way
to greet or come together,
but the good ideas begin like Jesus,
who watches with deep care,
and then changes
his own location and gate
to stand beside those who need
both freedom and company.

Ecumenical Relations

Will the tongues of fire return, giving us
one tongue with which to hear and speak?
We have spent long enough in our armchairs,
building cases for what is better or right.

It is time to come as guests to each other's houses,
to worship with language our mouths do not know
so we cannot not interrupt the beauty
or criticize what we've refused to understand.

It is time to get curious about one another
as holy traditions and as people of faith,
and to hold space for others to come
and get lost in what makes our own habits strange.

It is time to gather together, hair pulled back,
expecting a wind to blow and flames to consume
what we were so certain mattered most, to receive
a fresh word that gives us back to each other.

Interfaith Connections

We have been formed with a bias
for curiosity and belonging that can manifest
either as sacred interest or tense tribalism.

Christians have misunderstood
faithfulness as certainty in what we already have,
grace as a gift that whispers conditions,
interfaith dialogue as purely academic.

But there are holy pleasures waiting
in every tradition and scripture, to amplify
our awe and wonder for the divine,
to stretch what you thought could be true.

God bless your exploration, your relationships,
your open hearts willing to be changed by
the wideness of God's active mercy,
the myriad faces of God's image,
the strength of love that stretches
beyond a single tradition.

Stolen Land

This blessing begins with the land underfoot.
You have a story to tell,
a quiet theology of creation and despair
you have been singing and praying
for generations who are unwilling to listen.

We sit with you and marvel
at the power beneath our bodies;
you are a holy source, resourced
without much consideration at all.

SPEAK IT PLAIN

We sit with you and listen
to ancient progress and struggle,
tenacity rumbles beneath the imperial curse,
earth choked, gasping and breathing still!

We sit with you and confess
our economic transactions and waste,
all the time spent resisting a relationship
and spiritual adoration for this place.

We sit with you and all of these things
beyond discomfort and into the fullness of grief,
into the beginning of repair.

And then we give thanks for you and sing praise
to the God whose image is all around,
whose love is poured into each atom and breath
alive in the fabric of this very land.

For Moments

Accompaniment

There is urgency rising
in search of the right thing to say
or a way to fix what is hard or hurting.

But the Spirit is pulling you gently back
to stay in the sorrow and wait in the mystery
of being together without all the answers.

Just be here, she whispers.
It is enough.
It is more than enough.

After a Mass Shooting

It has happened again.
We feign disbelief, but
if we are being honest,
we can believe it. We must,
since this hate is born of us.

Each time our hearts break and feel
the suffering like a wave, but
then the passages cauterize,
closing off so we can live
with ourselves again.

There is a fear that flows
through the veins of this nation,
depressed in the souls of men and
unleashed on the bodies of innocents.
It rumbles between each gunshot.

It will continue to rage,
stealing breath and beats
from God's beloved
to power the terror
that is still weaving through
the maze of our dead-end hearts.

A New Year

This blessing knows how expectations heap
when something new begins, so it will stay airy
like frosting atop the pile of prospects.

And it will settle down into the crust
and depths of unseen fears and failures.

It will weave its way into hopeful forecasts
and good intentions so that you find grace
in every morsel of this new beginning set before you.

Anointing Another

The world is never finished
making plans for your life,
details to distract
from the quiet persistence of a call to
show up with love and speak it plain.

You hear yourself called
less than and *not quite*,
until you are worn down by
the scarcity of it all.

Its volume does not make it
loving or true.

But then
a voice finds you in the turbulence,
like the warm tone of a mother bird's song,
the sound that was there before everything else,
that croons each time you hunger or frighten:

I know you.
I love you.
You are mine.

Be gathered into safety and life
by the voice that calls
your true nature and name
guiding you back to yourself and your neighbor,
and the God who makes all things one.

Community Organizing

This work is quenched by the deepest wells
of curiosity and the satisfaction of trusting
we already know and love each other.

Organizing people is messy and never done,
like brushing your teeth while eating chocolate candy.

But you are seeing people
who have been waiting to be seen.

And you are piecing back together values
we have wielded as mere fragments.

Drink deeply and receive hospitality.
Ask gorgeous and genuine questions.
Shake the dust off your shoes and keep moving.

Courage

The world is filled
with good reasons to hide,
to turn away or inward to preserve
some distance and dignity.

But the struggle remains,
and justice beckons your attention
to come alive and together
for the here and now.

The Spirit of God stirs, even in fear,
so you might keep moving through
thresholds with hearts wide open
to heaven revealed in good courage.

Family before the Funeral

The tasks of death have been loud
these first days of absence,
a hurried stillness without your person.

There are people to greet.
They offer their consolation, but even
good intentions can be exhausting.

In the midst of these things,
there is rest and worship together.
We remember life and pray there is more.

There is room here for every single
truth and emotion, the full complexity
of grieving a person known so well.

Listen for the mourning and laughter
sprinkled on the stories while food is shared,
and a constellation of your person comes into view.

This is Holy Saturday, these days
between the cross and the empty tomb.
In the midst of grief and mystery,
while the tasks of death busy your hands,
Jesus is near, doing something brand new.

Gathering as a Semblance

God, we gather as a semblance of your people
divided and distracted
by the things we want to win,
the lists to which we tend,
the people we aim to love.

And though it is still morning,
we have already felt afraid or lonely,
we have already bartered with the world,
we have already grazed against disappointment
in systems, neighbors, and self.

SPEAK IT PLAIN

We gather as a semblance of your people
scarred by the blunt force of scarcity,
sneaking and striving for our fair share,
and then some.

God, we gather as a semblance of your people
with a twinge of apology,
for we look like mere remnants of your delight.
And yet these pieces are your pieces.
You have been known to create
order from chaos,
to decide with a breath that we are very good.

We gather as a semblance of your people
to hear your voice
move through the fear and isolation
with a familiar declaration too often misplaced:

We are loved.
We belong.
We are useful to you.

And since it is still morning,
there is light to guide us further together,
because morning no longer threatens
our sense of time and worth.

Now it is a warm and gracious vantage of your Spirit,
the One who helps us hear heaven
tearing in with a word that can
make a semblance whole.

Going to Camp

These are days for outdoor voices,
long sprints, and splashes
that sweat and cool like freedom.

These are nights for wild noises
and the crackle of bright campfires,
eyes that find heaven's starry banner above.

These are the foods, songs, and spaces
that help stick faith to our bones,
that locate God's love so near after all.

These are good ways to practice rejoicing,
to notice Christ in mud on your feet
and on the face of friends with flashlights
and the steady buzz of a bug in your ear.

This life is a gift. This faith is an adventure.
Blessed are you, who explore with awe.

Healthy Boundaries

It is a spiritual discipline to hold space
and set bounds for the sake of the whole.

Just because you can
doesn't mean you should.

You are called to some things,
not all the things.

Love does not mean fixing another
or losing your own well-being.

This burden is not your headstone,
for Jesus already died for these things.

You are one person, one day at a time.
And that is more than enough.

Home Communion

This is the meal
that does not end,
that moves from table to hands,
to bodies beyond.

This is the meal
that teaches enough,
to share and break and bless
like we are bits of heaven.

This is the meal
through which time can move,
linking loves lost and not yet
with bread and wine to satisfy.

This is the meal
that comes out to meet you,
stretching and squinting at a reunion
in the small of your hand.

This is the meal
that gives you strength,
and proclaims your place
at the longest table of all.

Hospice Care

We spend our lives searching for
dignity, belonging, and purpose.
May you know these things now.

Your decision is not a giving in
or a failure to thrive, but a celebration
of the dignity you found in this life.

Your community and caregivers
go with you into hospice as a testimony
to your belonging and value to many.

Your comfort and peace are new purpose,
for God enters our weakness to provide strength
and healing for everyone who awaits newness of life.

Infertility

There are too many stories in Scripture
about God closing and opening wombs,
about women made vulnerable by patriarchy's rules,
about families waiting without a promise to hold.

SPEAK IT PLAIN

If the women had written these stories,
they would sound like mourning cries and courage.

We would know how they comforted one another
and that they gathered where shame didn't dare follow.

We would have more songs for grief and longing,
more holy words for anger and hope.

They weren't written down,
but they are real, and God has heard them all.

So sing and wail and watch the moon,
and God will too, because your voice and body
are prophetic power and beauty
and life worthy of heaven's full attention.

Leaders Feeling Stuck

Being church
can feel like a traffic jam.
The crowd is pressed in,
inching along.

It gets hot and loud
when you are stuck,
between where you have been
and where you are meant to go.

The call is to find a view beyond
the stagnant limitations of this route,
to bet there is a way through or around
what is so hopelessly compressed these days.

Pray and hasten on, always trusting
there is more ground to cover,
and there will soon be speed that sends
fresh wind through the open windows.

Loss

You do your best
to hold love lightly,
palms open to the gift
for however long
it is meant to linger here.

But then wind threatens,
ruffling feathers,
sending a bolt of preservation,
closing your fierce fists,
so you cannot let go.

The time to hold these things
is fast and fleeting, yet
the loss endures
in leisure you come to resent
and then compels as friendship.

It might fool you into thinking
this breaking is rare, but then
the wind picks up again,
gathering those who also know
and those who gather anyway.

You do your best
to hold love lightly,
and then you mourn well,
because it is all very real,
and you are not alone.

Making Medical Decisions

May this blessing meet you in the long pauses
between choices or treatments or discussions of care.

If you are searching for one right answer,
know that you are the right one to answer.

If you are afraid of what happens next,
believe that the next thing can survive your fear.

There are a lot of right ways to tend this body and mind,
to provide good care and grab hold of life abundant.

You are doing the best you can with what you know.
And that is all this moment is asking of you.

Money Talk

Jesus did not shy away
from things that cause us shame,
the tools of bondage and conditions
that fracture our moral imagination.

Jesus spoke of money and debt
without a hint of shy apology, because
he came to release the captive,
to proclaim good news to the poor.

Jesus told stories of holy generosity
that seemed extravagant, even wasteful,
because they did not worry about defining fair,
instead rejoicing in the surprise of enough.

Jesus paid taxes to Caesar
without argument or loophole,
turned tables with hot hands
and righteous anger, declaring:

There will be no barriers
between the people and God,
no debt, burnt offering, or sacrifice worthy
of your fear or separation of life and freedom.

So speak of money and debt
because they are not to be feared any longer.
They are gifts and tools so long as
they do not separate, shame, or steal you away
from the moral imagination of God's Holy Spirit,
freedom, and life.

Moving into the Unknown

You can see only dimly,
squinting and straining,
seeking beyond the foreground
you built to feel more certain
about how this works.

You have been tempted
to hold onto the stuff right here
because you have developed
an allergy to the unknown
and unknowable, things off track.

But God never asked for certainty,
and you may never find it.
So instead this blessing offers
clarity about a few things
and holy curiosity for the rest.

You do not need to know
in order to move forward.
The pillar of cloud and fire
will find you out there,
stumbling around and discovering.

Planting a Garden

Before there was a temple,
there was a garden.
The rivers flowed
and the trees blossomed with fruit,
and there was more than enough
for everyone.

God is calling you back to the garden,
or into one wider than the first,
back into relationship with the earth,
back into the wild places
where you remember you are a creature
and food is miraculous
and there is plenty.

If you listen carefully,
you can hear God calling
in the hum of pollinators.
You can see God moving
in the migration of monarchs.
You can smell God blooming
in the herbs and harvest promise.

Come outside the temple, creatures.
Remember who you are and whose you are
by kneeling in the soil and tending what is good.

Planting a Memorial Tree

You are not only here,
grounded by gravity,
beating and breathing
and walking among the living.

You also are rooted
beneath what is easy to see,
tangled and nourished by the deep
stillness of earth that rumbles and rests.

There is wisdom buried
deep in the dirt,
in the dust of our ancestors,
in the spirit of the soil.

Look down to remember well
and give thanks for the stories that rest
in the company of creation,
still feeding you with more than you know.

And then look up to the highest branches
and even through them,
where wind blows and leaves dance
one moment, one season at a time.

There is joy that stirs beyond
your fingers stretched way up above,
mysteries that swirl just out of reach
and promises whispered in your ears.

You are filled with this breath
that comes all the way down,
that fills this realm, that raises dust
and the hairs on your neck.

You are not only here,
at the inseam of roots and sky,
but everywhere love is reposed
and blossoms and gathers you in.

God of life, we plant this tree with gratitude
for the life and ministry of [Name],
as act of resistance in the face of death,
as a sign of our hope and trust in your resurrection promise.
Come near to us in our remembering,
in the slow seasons of growth and change,
in our generations of becoming.
We ask for your presence through Jesus,
who has dwelled among us,
and the Holy Spirit, who refines and shapes us
with breath from heaven. Amen.

Political or Civic Grief

Tragedy has the power to shock your body
into isolation, to hide you away and apart
in deep grief or self-preservation
while waiting for an undoing or a miracle.

Your spirit has a magnetic pull.
It can brave the fragments
of your loneliness and fear, always
in search of others and wholeness.

You are gathered by the Spirit,
who teaches every spirit to move
together with courage and empathy,
even and especially today.

This holy house is called sanctuary,
a safe place, for bodies and spirits,
your despair and your hope,
both loud lamentation and songs of praise.

There must be enough room here
for the minor melodies, the weeping,
the sighs too deep for words—
the fullness of tragedy and your fragments.

Here we speak of hate and fear,
the unruly powers of this world,
for their destructive power and lies
woven through human story.

And here we speak of mercy and love,
the audacity of God's grace that is balm
in the cracks of our suffering, filling
that space between us with a final word
that is always Life.

Pregnancy or Infant Loss

This blessing unravels without guidance or permission.
It tumbles and ribbons into the heartbreak and cramps
of this traumatic loss, into the corners of aching,
the places that already and fiercely miss holding new life.

This blessing needs no slumber.
It will keep you company in the quiet sorrow of night,
when you wonder whether you ever will sleep to dream again.
It will keep watch if you drift off, and help hold everything terrible.

This blessing will whisper when you are ready
that you are a good parent, and this little one has been blessed
for a lifetime of weeks wrapped in your care,
which will be real and alive and for you both forever.

Sending a Group

For safety
in the midst of what is still unknown.

For joy and laughter
as memories pour a foundation.

For respite
from life's daily tasks and demands.

May you bless those you meet
with grace and humility.

May your hearts be willing,
changed by the challenge that finds you.

May you feel gratitude
for what is asked of your faith in Jesus,
who sends and guides you with love. Amen.

Taking a Sabbatical

It is only human
to become what you do,
to believe you are necessary
for good order and momentum.

So in the beginning God set humankind apart
on a planet that moves without your control,
that revolves despite your wild desire
to be at the very center of things.

God promised provision on the seventh day,
so that you could practice resistance to
your zealous rhythms with rest,
so that you could stop for a season and trust:

I am so small.
And also,
I matter so much.

It is here in the absence of doing
you will remember the terrible and wonderful news—
that God is still here, making things new,
even and often without your help.

May this Sabbath time return your identity
from production to relationship in which
you hear the call to some things, not all the things,
and relish your place as a creature of God.

Veterans

You answered a call that set you apart,
that required your body and mind,
that shaped your faith and knows your spirit,
that knit you into an intense kinship
even death cannot put asunder.

For the ways your memories and trauma remain,
we honor you with the vigil of our love.
For the sacrifices civility cannot comprehend,
we tend to your untold stories with presence and care.
For the reconciliation you may not find in the church,
we will hold space for what you know and need in your being.

May the peace of God, which surpasses all understanding,
guard your heart and mind through Christ Jesus.
And may the membership of Christ's body
be made wide for the fullness of your story,
all you have suffered and all you keep offering
in the name of liberty and justice for all.

Waiting Together

Tie this blessing around your wrist,
and we will do the same.
For we are bound by hope shared
and grace measured beyond
what one can carry alone.

It will fray and tangle and remain
with stubborn courage, until
the thing we carry together
does not seem so heavy anymore.

Welcoming Guests on Holidays

Christendom still flickers,
just barely, on high holy days,
when obligation and family tradition
hang thick in the sanctuary air.
They do not come often, but still they come.

Meet them with joy and wonder,
since they have been called by the story
to gather with the ghosts of those
who first told them about the manger and tomb,
to linger near the news they long to hear
even now, even here.

Welcome them home
with delight the world does not offer,
with grace that surprises expectations,
with love that makes the presence of God
startle souls in all the best ways.

2

For the Seasons

The seasons of the church have stretched me to live in both chronological and *kairos* time, marking the mysteries of God at work in my life with colors, stories, and permission for all kinds of spiritual moods that inform my faith.

The deep blues of Advent and Mary's Song hold space for my wonder in a season that tells me to hustle for sales and decor. I look for stories about God showing up in the darkness of night to whisper a call, change someone's heart, and extend grace. It is a season for challenging the harmful and racist narrative that light is good and dark is evil with stories about the safe and sacred darkness of Mary's womb or the holy dreams that came to Joseph in the middle of the night.

Consider using the poetry in this section for staff devotions or as readings in worship. Use language to help your community connect these ancient seasons and festivals with their daily lives. They still have something hard and good to say to our worship and work after all these years.

Advent

The sacred call "Prepare!"
does not ask for lists or logistics.
We do not "Keep awake!" only to ensure
we are not forgotten at the rapture.
Nor is the stillness sedentary.

So do not simply go looking
for a candle scent to capture
what it means to Ponder,
or a gift to prove your Love,
or a tall tree to announce,
"Joy to the World!"

Advent lays bare visions of time bending
into already and not yet,
by the God who tears apart
the hustle, the heavens, the temple curtain!
with no intention of mending
back together our favored boundaries.

This is the thin space where
stillness is powerful and
God is changing our hearts,
so sacred Ponder, Love, and Joy
can birth and shelter.

The miracle grows with slow strength
in the one place we have all called home,
where we do not yet know another way,
while our fullness is being prepared,
carried, and nourished by
the One who says, "Yes."

Saint Lucia Day

We light a candle to remember
it doesn't take much.
A small flame
can make shadows dance
and eyes twinkle,
casting a warm glow
on those we love.

John's Gospel begins
with the promise of light
that darkness cannot overcome.
Though it pulls the sun lower,
it does not have the last word!

We cannot always see
where we are going, but
there is enough light
to illumine our bodies,
drawn together by both
the night and the light.

There is enough
to make us wonder—
is this a glimpse
of heaven's light that is
already and not yet on the way?

We grin as the wax drips,
giving itself to the light,
and for a moment we know why
God came down:

In the darkness
we are so very beautiful.

Blue Christmas

this is the time
when things get loud,
when hope gets muffled
and fears abound.

FOR THE SEASONS

this is the time
when we gather together
heaping expectation,
judgment, and laughter,
hiding the longing,
the ache, and disaster.

this is the time
when we're fiercely surrounded,
but feel lonesome
and foolish
or haunted, confounded.

this is the time
where the loudest is cheer,
while weary shame lingers right here.

but that is not Truth, you precious, beloved:
we are all hiding, all longing, all living with judgment.
we are all breaking, wondering where we belong,
and whether there is room for us inside the song.

so put down the list and lean into the grief,
and trust that you are not merely songless belief.
you are messy and worthy—
made perfectly whole
by the One who rubs balm on the cracks of your soul,
by the One who saves nations with love crescendos.

this is the time
the whole world is blue!
and Jesus is coming to make the pain new
to strip it of power
to banish all fear
so that life—life abundant—can boldly appear.

this is the time
for your blue to be known
and lived by a God who has hay on the throne
and sung by a scrappy church choir your own
and loved by the babe who makes blue his home.

Day of Epiphany

Long ago, Christians began celebrating
the magi arriving in Bethlehem.
Watching the sky and following stars
set their minds on heavenly things.

The light held power that changed their course,
and opened their dreams
to more beauty and justice
than the earth had ever known.

I wish to begin this new year by celebrating
the possibilities beyond my own earthly will,
to watch the sky and follow the stars so that
I remember that we are all made
of heaven's own dreams.

The flames are dancing and warm
on this long winter night,
a sign of what could be the way,
and guide toward purpose and love
that threaten this world's callous comfort.

We mark the thresholds of home
with chalk like stardust
to remind us where to look
and how to travel with wonder.

Baptism of Our Lord

One Voice: The Israelites were guided through waters from slavery into freedom.
All: Like the crowds from Judea, Jesus was washed in the Jordan River.

One Voice: God called the Israelites a holy people and claimed them for good.
All: A voice came from heaven, "You are my Son, the Beloved One, with you I am well pleased."

One Voice: The Israelites wandered in the wilderness for forty years, learning to trust God and becoming a new people.

All: The Spirit thrust Jesus into the wilderness for forty days, where he was tempted by Satan, surrounded by earthly beasts and celestial beings.

One Voice: Israel emerged a nation, God's chosen people bound for the promised land.

All: Jesus came to Galilee proclaiming the good news, "The kingdom of God has come near!"

One Voice: Like Daniel, whose vision told of great beasts stirred by the winds and sea,

All: Jesus has devastating news for the political empires that oppress God's people: God's time is now.

One Voice: The prophet Isaiah once yearned, "Oh, that you would tear open the heavens and come down."

All: In baptism, God has done just that. The border has been broken open, beyond repair. Love has come!

Transfiguration Day

There are glimpses
in the thin places between our worlds,
where certainty gives way
to something else entirely.

FOR THE SEASONS

We want to linger in the warm glow of mystery,
the soft hum of all being well,
because the view is fair,
and the climb was all we had to offer.

But we do not glimpse the divine
thanks to our own struggle or deserving.
It is revealed by grace for a moment,
while we catch our breath and faith again.

Our figure is changed so that,
when we turn back down the mountain,
the glimpse might go with us and
warm those still waiting at the bottom.

Ash Wednesday

Tonight we remember
that we come from the dust
both earthen and cosmic
thanks to bursts of atoms
billions of years old,
still chasing
the coattails of *kairos*.

SPEAK IT PLAIN

We are the heavy elements:
carbon, nitrogen, oxygen,
pressed and held down
by the gravity of sin
trapped in the stillness,
waiting for nova until
wind, breath, spirit
fills the ordinary
and everywhere
with more.

Tonight we remember
that we come from the dust
by listening carefully
to the sound of our chests
rising and falling,
fragile with the wonder of dust
that lives.

Holy Saturday

The sky is still dark,
or maybe it has come
and gone again.
This is a vigil,
but not for Easter.

FOR THE SEASONS

Keeping time is tragic,
so we drift
in and out of sleep,
and puffy eyes observe
only the piles of ointment
and death clothes
stacked and weary
near the back door.

Maybe you can
decorate and bake,
but some of us can only wait
in the silence between
what is already and not yet.
These are holy hours
to consider how far
God is willing to go
for love.

The Easter Season

Fifty days for impossible,
unlikely encounters,
signs of new life,
creative resilience,
and speechless joy.

Fifty days for scars shown,
real human bodies
alive, telling stories
about what has hurt
and been made whole.

Fifty days for peace enfleshed,
moving through locked doors,
down dirt roads,
and on the beach
smoking fish to eat for breakfast.

Fifty days for Spirit breathed,
forgiveness unleashed,
presence that's pure,
courage that finds us
together for good.

Fifty days for jubilee,
debts fully repaid,
broken life restored,
people rejoicing
and raised from the dead!

FOR THE SEASONS

Ascension Day

It could have been a magic trick,
a one-man show:
Now you see me, now you don't.
But this rising has been a gift
for the whole of creation.

We have put our finger in his scars
and felt the breath of peace.
We have recognized him calling our name
and in the breaking bread.
He joined us on the road
and cooked breakfast on the fire.

Our senses know something has changed,
and it will not be kept in isolation.
So when he gives us to each other,
when he goes to prepare a place for us,
there is good reason to hope:
We will all be together in paradise.

Pentecost

There is a candle near the altar
that glows without rest.
Its flame dances in the hurricane,
safe and silent while we sleep.

Or is it?
This light is bold enough,
with or without us, to start a fire
where there was only dust and fear.

It flickers now, casting a glow
in the dim stillness of what we build,
the places we hide and wait for certain
signs of what will still be.

Perhaps this fire is waiting
on a wind so we can see
like our ancestors
a burning bush, a pillar of fire,
a burnt offering ablaze
with life that speaks.

Breathe deeply, church.
You are the wind
you are waiting for,
and the time has come

to kindle and flare
like tongues dancing,
like wax that drips without reserve,
melting and molding for the luminous

Holy Trinity Sunday

Let's forget for today
the urge to sort God out
with formula or creed.

Let this be a field trip
to dance in the throne room,
to squeeze in among angels
and sing with wonder
that does not need proving.

Let those holies resound
in that shining hall, and we'll smile
because there is enough,
and mystery does not need solving,
only adoration and company
with the One
who was and is and will be
even still.

Let's forget for today
we prefer knowing for certain,
and instead rejoice
in the fullness of love.

(Extra) Ordinary Time

There is a season
that stretches like the days,
long and green until
you think there's only this
one way of being alive.

There are prayers for sun and rain.
What we have planted bears fruit
and the gardens grow wild,
making us share and reminding:
There is enough after all.

When you dive into the lake
or wade with your legs in the river,
the cold water steals your breath
and your baptism comes to mind.

For the Seasons

When you pack sandwiches and wine
and feast with neighbors and crickets
in the grass at sunset, and the meal is enough
with baskets left over, remember the supper.

These are ordinary times, of course,
but they are also extraordinary,
filled with promises that follow you
to the ends of the earth and back again.

Reformation Day

It was a perfect storm,
resistance in spades thanks to
politicians with power,
artists with patrons,
a press for printing
still new to the masses.

The church reformed
in the public square,
where real people protested
with low approval ratings,
asking real questions and pushing
on church to meet them outside
in the mess of the day.

It is a perfect storm,
resistance in spades thanks to
rising generations calling
the church to step out from behind
its mighty fortress
for the sake of real people
and real questions
and the mess of today.

Come outside, church,
with eyes to see and ears to listen.
This is a perfect storm
of politic and art,
language and freedom,
inspired by heaven's refining
and a reforming song that is
both ancient and new.

All Saints' Day

I listen for it tolling
from steeples in the sky.

The bells stir the air
between here and heartache.
For a moment,
the mystery satisfies, and
we are all together.

FOR THE SEASONS

I hang onto memories and promises
with my fingernails
just barely—
not because I am certain,
but because it is all that's left.
Because if I let go, I will fall
and break apart.

Perhaps
someone will speak
of my Beloved today
and then I will not be so alone.
Hearing the name aloud
makes it real,
shares the weight
like a new song I think
I've always known.

There are candles to light
the quiet resistance of remembering.

CHRIST THE KING

We dare to declare that
Christ is King
on the eve of a new year
in the life of the church.
Such simple proclamation,
and yet easily forgotten.
So central to our faith,
and yet dangerous to speak
in the shadow of empires.

Christ is King,
the patriarchy is not.
Christ is King,
white supremacy is not.
Christ is King,
democracy is not.
Christ is King,
big money is not.
Christ is King,
the status quo is not.
Christ is King,
the church is not.
Christ is King,
and I am not.

FOR THE SEASONS

It rings in our ears
like auld lang syne—
Christ is King!
The last and truest word of all.

Section II

Liturgies, Litanies, and Special Services

The following five chapters contain material intended to be used within gatherings that call for group response. To help you facilitate the full use of these liturgies, litanies, and special services, a code is provided on page 186 of this book. Use this code to access the material in these chapters and to make copies to suit your particular needs. Purchase of this book comes with permission to make copies for use in your setting.

3
The Church Confesses

We often begin Christian worship with a leader up front who invites the assembly to confess their sins before God and neighbor. The idea is that we cannot sing and pray and receive the supper with honest hearts until we have told the truth about ourselves. And that's a beautiful thing.

But sometimes we need to hear the institutional church reflect and apologize. The church has been declaring the importance of confession week after week for thousands of years, so why isn't the church better at embodying this? Are we too ashamed or stubborn to make a searching and fearless moral inventory of ourselves? Are we unwilling to begin repairing what has been broken? Are we afraid mercy will not apply?

I have spent seasons in the pews unable to participate in this portion of the liturgy, not because I thought myself blameless, but because I did not trust the church with my confession. I could only hear the hypocrisy of an institution telling me the power of repentance, reparations, and reconciliation while I could see no real evidence of the system practicing what it preached. That part of the liturgy hurt my body and spirit, reminding me that the acknowledgment and apologies I longed for might never come.

The Christian church has shamed bodies, harbored predators, annihilated cultures, benefited from racism, and protected its own power instead of the people God calls us to serve. The church has caused bloodshed, broken spirits, and blamed victims. For all of its faithful, inspired, and holy work, the body of Christ is made of real people and has plenty to confess about fear, shame, and sin.

This section calls the institutional church to confess: to God, to its many parts, and to the people and places it has caused harm. My own faith has been healed by bearing witness to these confessions from a place in the pews. My leadership has been strengthened while standing with colleagues, together breaking the silence and handing over something true and vulnerable about the church. Our stories are varied, our stoles are colorful, and our spirits are unified by the desire to begin worship with guts and grace. As though we are really dying and rising. As though forgiveness is real.

There will be people in the assembly who need to receive this confession more than they need to give it, having been uniquely hurt by these very sins. Before leading these confessions in worship, make clear that participation is, of course, an invitation and not mandatory. Consider offering thanks to God for the people who are able to attend worship in spite of being harmed by the institution and asking comfort for those who do not feel safe or welcome in worship at all.

The Church Confesses: For Sexual Shame

Living God, we have come to offer public apology
for the way your holy church benefits
from a repressed sexual ethic at the expense of God's people.
A brief silence.
We confess that we have taught human sexuality
in ways that have promoted shame and embarrassment
instead of power and beauty.
We are truly sorry and humbly repent.
We confess that we have misused the gospel of Jesus
to decimate cultures and languages around the world,
and to condone oppression, racism, and misogyny for generations.
We are truly sorry and humbly repent.
We confess that we have heard God's creation of male and female
as a binary set, one or the other, exclusive and simple,
which has underestimated the beautiful spectrum of God's image
and condoned homophobia, transphobia, and biphobia.
We are truly sorry and humbly repent.
We confess that we have pitted the fullness and mystery
of God's creative image against its own self,
discerning beauty and value according to
the social norms of patriarchy instead of the teachings of Jesus.
We are truly sorry and humbly repent.

We confess that we have too often described
the feminine helper in Genesis as a foolish temptress,
responsible for the sins of men and less than equal.
We are truly sorry and humbly repent.
We confess the limitations of our lectionaries
and the insufficient time we spend
with women and their stories in worship and study.
We are truly sorry and humbly repent.
We confess the purity culture that narrows and simplifies
the virtue of women and femmes to their chastity,
and sexualizes girls from a young age.
We are truly sorry and humbly repent.
We confess that our institutions and systems
have been complicit in protecting predators
in families, churches, schools, and communities.
We are truly sorry and humbly repent.
We confess that we have kept silent when oppressed people
have asked the body of Christ to say something with compassion,
and to do justice and mercy with our power.
We are truly sorry and humbly repent.
We confess, on behalf of the whole Christian church,
that some of our history, our theology, and our leadership
have caused people on the margins pain and suffering,
that we have chosen the status quo of our systems
over protecting God's beloved people.
We are truly sorry and humbly repent.

For these things and more, we are truly sorry and humbly repent.
May the church repent more boldly in these days,
daring to practice what we preach,
embodying humility in a proud and aching world,
learning to trust that grace might be real for us, too.
Amen.

> Did you know that your body
> is a temple and the Holy Spirit is alive in you?
> You are valuable and your body
> belongs to God's good care.
> —Inspired by 1 Corinthians 6:19–20

THE CHURCH CONFESSES: FOR WHITE SUPREMACY

Living God, we have come to offer public apology
for the ways your holy church benefits
from white supremacy and racism
at the expense of God's people.
A brief silence.
Merciful God,
> **Your son Jesus came into human form,**
> **sheltered by the womb and arms**
> **of a young unwed mother,**
> **a baby, a boy, a man with brown skin,**

**migrated as a refugee and immigrant,
considered a common tradesman,
deemed a threat by his own government,
and lynched to death on a tree.**

**This is how you chose to reveal
heaven's beauty and power in the world.**

**And yet we whitewash this story
with our stained-glass windows
and our illustrated children's Bibles,
with our single stories and stereotypes
about Africa and the Middle East,
with American history written to satisfy
the empire's point of view.**

We confess the ways our institutions and leaders
have sanitized the life and death of Jesus,
telling a far less offensive and radical story
about God's love for people on the margins,
domesticating the words and ways of Jesus
to preserve the comfort and power of some.

    Turn us from evil to your goodness, O God.

We confess the harm done by the church
in the name of Jesus Christ;
the wars funded, the pillaged wealth,
the cruelty of colonization,
the cultures dehumanized and decimated,
the abuse hidden from justice.

    Turn us from evil to your goodness, O God.

We confess the misinterpretations of Scripture,
the gospel abused to condone genocide and slavery,
to condemn the LGBTQIA+ community,
to keep women from leadership,
to confuse nationalism with faith in Christ.
Turn us from evil to your goodness, O God.
We confess the church's part in white fragility,
an unwillingness to repair and reconcile
on the terms of those so gravely hurt,
while systems of oppression continue to mutate
from generation to generation.
Turn us from evil to your goodness, O God.
We confess our faith in whiteness,
the superiority that white people
are taught to both wield and deny,
the quiet and persistent racism
that informs too much of who we are
and how we show up in the world.
Turn us from evil to your goodness, O God.
We confess the racial segregation of the church,
our naive explanations and solutions
that expect assimilation before belonging,
and the historical and political conversations
we avoid while our children are listening,
learning what matters to God and to the church.
Turn us from evil to your goodness, O God.

We confess our faith in a zero-sum game,
the fear of being overcome,
the grief in losing dominance,
the firm grip on the pen that writes history
in familiar and favorable terms.
Turn us from evil to your goodness, O God.
We confess that we practice our faith
by avoiding this open wound,
as if it will heal itself in time.
We prefer this artificial unity
to the voice of Jesus,
who told us to reconcile before all the rest:

> If you are offering your gift
> at the altar of the Lord and
> remember that there is brokenness
> and unfinished business between you and
> your sibling, stop. Put down your gift.
> God will wait while you turn around and
> find your sibling. Listen, confess, repair, reconcile, and restore that relationship.
> Then come back to the altar of the Lord and offer your gift.
> —Inspired by Matthew 5:23–24

The Church Confesses: For Self-Preservation

Living God, we have come to offer public apology
for the way your holy church worships its own preservation,
clings to mortal power, and resists transformation by your Spirit.
A brief silence.
Merciful God,
> you put on flesh and lived among us,
> showing all of creation how
> to hold this world lightly,
> to lose ourselves,
> to trust that death is not the end after all.
>
> And yet we struggle
> to practice what we preach,
> hiding behind locked doors,
> frozen by fear of loss and change.

We confess the ways our institutions and systems
have protected the powerful instead of the powerless,
have denied and hidden sin instead of confessing it,
have caused violence and oppression
instead of peace and liberation.
> **Have mercy on us, O God.**

We confess the wars funded,
the pillaged wealth,
the cruelty of colonization,
the sacred and beautiful cultures decimated,
all in the name of Christ.
   Have mercy on us, O God.
We confess how often the church
has been absent from the public square,
has hesitated to speak truth to power,
has prioritized the emotions of majority
over the safety and dignity of the minority.
   Have mercy on us, O God.
We confess our fear of being changed
by death and resurrection,
our firm grip on our own ways,
our dangerous adoration
for what we have built on earth.
   Have mercy on us, O God.
We confess the ways we exclude our neighbors
by clinging to what already has perished,
unwilling to make space for newness and life.
   Have mercy on us, O God.
We confess that we prefer
our slow denial and dissolution
and a false sense of control
to the voice of Jesus, who speaks it plain:

THE CHURCH CONFESSES

If you're going to follow me,
let go of who you have been,
the power you've had,
your definition of success,
your aspirational sense of self.
Gather the things that are real
and come with me.
Because if you spend this life
trying to save it, you will lose it.
But if you let go of this life
for my sake, you will finally find it.
—Inspired by Matthew 16:24–25

4

Celebrating Baptism

Celebrating baptism during worship services means the family and friends of the baptized show up, guests who carry a variety of beliefs about salvation into the space. As worship leaders, we have an opportunity to make sure the good news doesn't get buried in ecclesiastical language or make exclusive assumptions. Let's teach people why we do what we do by showing them what matters—and who matters—to God.

My seminary education taught me the rules and regulations of sacramental ministry, but loving people in a particular context has been known to bend the systematic framework so grace can breathe and people can live abundantly. I once wrote an academic paper about why I wasn't supposed to baptize stillborn babies, but when my clinic's pager went off in the middle of the night, all bets were off. I could not decline the request from an undocumented immigrant, a Spanish-speaking Catholic woman desperate to do something faithful and parental for her still, sweet newborn. In that moment, none of those barriers mattered. I had been called to the bedside of a grieving mother who was asking for God's promises to be big enough.

This section includes resources for baptism and confirmation, but also a naming ceremony for our transgender siblings and a blessing for those who do not wish to affirm their baptism in accordance with the church and Grandma's timeline.

Do not let the wideness of God's mercy get lost in the shuffle of our liturgy or doctrine. By choosing water and the word, God takes care of the cosmic mystery and gives us the simple parts to tend with wonder. So teach as you go. Invite the kids in with tasks to keep their senses engaged. Model consent when holding or touching the newest members of your community. Weave their names and local bodies of water into your prayers for the day, giving thanks for their power and beauty. And be willing to admit what you do not know, what you cannot know, about the resurrection and the life in our midst.

Thanksgiving for Baptism

Blessed be the holy Trinity, + one God,
who creates, saves, and sends us
with love that lives forever.
Amen.

Joined to Christ in the waters of baptism,
we give thanks for the Great Exchange,
the mercy and forgiveness that wrap
our true selves in sacred belonging and purpose.
> **Thanks be to God. Alleluia!**

For a word at the dawn of creation,
which spoke water and life into being.
> **Thanks be to God. Alleluia!**

For the great flood that revealed nature's power
and God's commitment to life after death.
> **Thanks be to God. Alleluia!**

For the river that carried Moses safely,
building a bridge between mothers and nations.
> **Thanks be to God. Alleluia!**

For the rock split open in the desert,
spilling water for those thirsting for freedom.
> **Thanks be to God. Alleluia!**

For the One who turned water to wine
and met a woman at the well with living water.
> **Thanks be to God. Alleluia!**

For the gift of holy baptism,
which declares there are no more godforsaken places,
and nothing can separate us from the love of God in Jesus.
For Christ is risen!
> **Christ is risen, indeed. Alleluia!**

God of life, we rejoice with the waters that cover creation;
our songs of praise echo their dancing tides and streams.
Pour out your Holy Spirit on this community and all of creation.
Cleanse our fears. Drown our divisions.
Give us mercy and grace to drink so that our whole lives
are signs of death defeated and thirst quenched
thanks to the risen Jesus, the Son of God.
   Amen.

Baptizing a Child

Welcome in the name of God
who creates, saves, and calls us
with grace that lasts forever.
   Amen.
God's love and salvation in Jesus
can seem mysterious and cosmically far away,
so we give thanks for the sacrament of baptism,
which pulls these big promises down into the natural world.
Here, God's sacred time comes to play with our human time.
Baptism claims us by name on a specific day in history
and entangles every witness in the good news
of God's never-ending *Yes*.

God uses water to connect these sacred words
to our senses. This is a symbol we already know
for its creative power to help and nourish.
We use water to clean, bathe, cook, and play.

CELEBRATING BAPTISM

In baptism, we are claimed by the God of living water,
a precious and limitless supply
of that which gives and sustains life.

Parents/Guardians/Sponsors:
We present [child's name] to receive the sacrament of Holy Baptism.

As you bring [child's name] to receive the gift of baptism,
you are entrusted with responsibilities:

to live with them among God's faithful people,
to pray for them daily,
bring them to hear the word and share the Supper,
teach them the prayers, creeds, and commandments,
place in their hands the holy Scriptures,
and nurture them in faith and prayer
so they may learn to trust God,
proclaim Christ through word and deed,
care for others and the world God made,
and work for justice and peace.

Do you promise to help [child's name]
grow in the Christian faith and life?
If so, say, "We do!"

Parents/Guardians/Sponsors: **We do!**

If the child is able to make a verbal affirmation:
[Child's name], we are here to declare God's *yes* in your life
and so your family grows bigger thanks to all these people,
who promise to love and support you no matter what.

If the child is able and willing to participate verbally:
Do you wish to be baptized today? If so, say, "I do."
Child: **I do.**

Congregation, please rise.
We baptize in public worship
so the church can make promises to [child's name],
to speak these promises uniquely for [child's name],
and to mark this moment in our human experience.
We are gathered as one congregation,
but we are making these promises
on behalf of the whole Christian church
across time and space.

The world will waste no time telling [child's name]
lies about power, value, and love.
So we stand with this child [them] this morning,
one of many times,
to speak God's truth about these things.

People of God:
Do you reject the devil and all the forces that defy God,
the powers of this world that rebel against God,
and the ways of sin that pull us away from God?
If so, say, "We do!"
   We do!
Do you promise to speak the truth
about [child's name]'s identity as a child of God,
affirming them through all circumstances
with their first and forever name: Beloved?

Do you promise to hold healthy and safe space for them
to grow in faith believing there is nothing they can do
to make God love them any more or any less
than they already are loved in Jesus? If so, say, "We do!"
   We do!
Do you believe in God the Father?
I believe in God, the Father Almighty,
creator of heaven and earth.
Do you believe in Jesus Christ, the Son of God?
I believe in Jesus Christ, his only Son our Lord.
He was conceived by the power of the Holy Spirit
and born of the virgin Mary.
He suffered under Pontius Pilate,
was crucified, died, and was buried.
He descended into hell.
On the third day he rose again.
He ascended into heaven,
and is seated at the right hand of the Father.
He will come again to judge the living and the dead.
Do you believe in God the Holy Spirit?
I believe in the Holy Spirit, the holy catholic church,
the communion of saints, the forgiveness of sins,
the resurrection of the body, and the life everlasting.

There's nothing particularly special
about the water we're using today.
It came from the faucet and is just like the water
you drink when you're thirsty or use to bathe at home.

But this ordinary water becomes extraordinary,
because we know God can do amazing things with water.
There are lots of stories in the Bible about water
making things new, saving people, and sustaining life.
We know that when God makes promises with water,
amazing things can happen.

Let's pray together and remember some of these stories
about the power of water and God's promises.

Saving God,
we give you thanks for the waters of creation
that have nourished the earth since you spoke life into being.
We remember Noah and his family
rocking back and forth on the floodwaters,
Miriam keeping watch over her brother Moses in the Nile,
the Israelites fleeing through the spray of the Red Sea,
the thirsty drinks they took from water
that poured from a rock in the desert.
You sent your son to be carried
by the water and waves of Mary's womb,
to be baptized in the Jordan with the crowds,
to turn water into wine, to meet the Samaritan woman at the well,
to feel the thirst of humanity in life and death.
Rain down your Spirit so that, by this water and your word,
we are renewed by the gifts of Jesus and the truth about love.
    Amen.

[Child's name], I baptize you in the name of
the Father, and of the Son, and of the Holy Spirit,
one God and Mother of us all. **Amen.**

Gracious God,
through Jesus, you have destroyed the power of death!
And, since death isn't so scary anymore,
we are set free to live with courage and abundance.
Bless [name] with dignity, belonging, and purpose from heaven.
Pour out your Holy Spirit upon [name],
the spirit of wisdom and understanding,
the spirit of counsel and might,
the spirit of knowledge and the fear of the Lord,
the spirit of joy in your presence. **Amen.**

[*Name*], beloved child of God,
you have been sealed by the Holy Spirit
and marked with the cross of Christ forever.

Sponsors light the baptismal candle from the Christ candle and hold it up for all to see.

Parents/Guardians/Sponsors:
[Name], you are a new creation in Christ!
See? Everything old has passed away, and you are brand new.
Be reconciled to God and a blessing in this world.

[Child's name], we just heard your family, the church, and God
make a big promise, the truest thing of all:
You are saved by the grace of God, whether you like it or not.
When you forget that, we'll all be here to remind you.
After all, we share a spirit now, which means we're in this together.

O God, the giver of all life,
look with kindness on [parents'/guardians' names].
Let them ever rejoice in the gift you have given them.
Guide them as teachers and examples of faithfulness
for [child's name] and strengthen them
in their own baptismal promises.
Use the members of this congregation
and the whole body of Christ to support them
through prayer, love, and hospitality so that
they continue to grow in love toward you and all of creation.
Amen.

Please welcome our newest sibling in Christ, [child's name].

Baptizing an Adult

Welcome in the name of God
who creates, saves, and calls us
with grace that lasts forever.
Amen.

CELEBRATING BAPTISM

God's love and salvation in Jesus
can seem mysterious and cosmically far away,
so we give thanks for the sacrament of baptism,
which pulls these big promises down into the natural world.
Here, God's sacred time comes to play with our human time.
Baptism claims us by name on a specific day in history
and entangles every witness in the good news
of God's never-ending *yes*.

God uses water to connect these sacred words
to our senses. This is a symbol we already know
for its creative power to help and nourish.
We use water to clean, bathe, cook, and play.

In baptism, we are claimed by the God of living water,
a precious and limitless supply
of that which gives and sustains life.

[Name], do you desire to be baptized into the body of Christ,
to hear publicly that you are a beloved child of God,
to be surrounded by promises that will nurture your faith?
If so, say, "I do."

Baptismal candidate: **I do.**

As you come to receive the gift of baptism,
you are entrusted with responsibilities:

to live among God's faithful people,
to pray daily,
to receive the word of God and the holy Supper,
to learn the prayers, creeds, and commandments,
to open the holy Scriptures,
to be nurtured by the faith and prayers of others,
so that you learn to trust God,
proclaim Christ through word and deed,
care for others and the world God made,
and work for justice and peace.

Do you promise to grow in the Christian faith and life?
If so, say, "I do."

Baptismal candidate: **I do.**

The gift of baptism is freely given by God
and does not depend on your own understanding or action.
As a member of the body of Christ,
you carry these promises together with a community.

People of God, do you promise to help [name]
grow in the Christian faith and life,
to be a living testament to God's *yes* and the wide family
we have in the church on earth? If so, say, "We do!"

Congregation/Sponsors: **We do!**

CELEBRATING BAPTISM

Congregation, please rise.
We baptize in public worship
so the church can make promises
and speak these promises uniquely for [name],
and to mark this moment in our human experience.
We are gathered as one congregation,
but we are making these promises
on behalf of the whole Christian church
across time and space.

The world spends plenty of time
telling us lies about power, value, and love.
But baptism speaks a different word.
Grace is a still, small voice that never tires
of pushing through our phony labels
with what's good and true and lasts forever.

Sponsors and people of God:
Do you reject the devil and all the forces that defy God,
the powers of this world that rebel against God,
and the ways of sin that pull us away from God?
If so, say, "We do!"
    We do!

Do you promise to speak the truth
about [name]'s identity as a child of God,
affirming them through all circumstances
with their first and forever name: Beloved?
If so, say, "We do!"
   We do!

Do you promise to hold healthy and safe space for [name]
to grow in faith, believing there is nothing they can do
to make God love them any more or any less
than they are already loved in Jesus?
If so, say, "We do!"
   We do!

Do you believe in God the Father?
I believe in God, the Father Almighty,
creator of heaven and earth.

Do you believe in Jesus Christ, the Son of God?
I believe in Jesus Christ, his only Son our Lord.
He was conceived by the power of the Holy Spirit
and born of the virgin Mary.
He suffered under Pontius Pilate,
was crucified, died, and was buried.
He descended into hell.
On the third day he rose again.
He ascended into heaven,
and is seated at the right hand of the Father.
He will come again to judge the living and the dead.

Do you believe in God the Holy Spirit?
I believe in the Holy Spirit, the holy catholic church, the communion of saints, the forgiveness of sins, the resurrection of the body, and the life everlasting.

There's nothing particularly special
about the water we're using today.
It came from the faucet and is just like the water
you drink when you're thirsty or use to bathe at home.

But this ordinary water becomes extraordinary,
because we know God can do amazing things with water.
There are lots of stories in the Bible about water
making things new, saving people, and sustaining life.
We know that when God makes promises with water,
amazing things can happen.

Let's pray together and remember some of these stories
about the power of water and God's promises.

Saving God,
we give you thanks for the waters of creation
that have nourished the earth since you spoke life into being.
We remember Noah and his family
rocking back and forth on the floodwaters,
Miriam keeping watch over her brother Moses in the Nile,
the Israelites fleeing through the spray of the Red Sea,
the thirsty drinks they took from water
that poured from a rock in the desert.
You sent your son to be carried
by the water and waves of Mary's womb,
to be baptized in the Jordan with the crowds,
to turn water into wine, to meet the Samaritan woman at the well,
to feel the thirst of humanity in life and death.
Rain down your Spirit so that, by this water and your word,
we are renewed by the gifts of Jesus and the truth about love.
    Amen.

[Name], I baptize you in the name of
the Father, and of the Son, and of the Holy Spirit,
one God and Mother of us all. **Amen.**

Gracious God,
through Jesus, you have destroyed the power of death!
And, since death isn't so scary anymore,
we are set free to live with courage and abundance.
Bless [name] with dignity, belonging, and purpose from heaven.
Pour out your Holy Spirit upon [name],

the spirit of wisdom and understanding,
the spirit of counsel and might,
the spirit of knowledge and the fear of the Lord,
the spirit of joy in your presence. **Amen.**

[Name], beloved child of God,
you have been sealed by the Holy Spirit
and marked with the cross of Christ forever.

Sponsors light the baptismal candle from the Christ candle and hold it up for all to see.

Sponsors: **[*Name*], you are a new creation in Christ!**
See? Everything old has passed away, and you are brand new.
Be reconciled to God and a blessing in this world.

[Name], you have heard this community declare
God's big promise, the truest thing of all:
You are saved by the grace of God, whether you like it or not.
When you forget that, we'll be here to remind you.
After all, we share a spirit now, which means we're in this together.

Please welcome our newest sibling in Christ, [name].

Congregation: **Welcome, [name]!**
We rejoice in your baptism
and promise to help you remember today.
Faith can get hard and heavy, so we carry it together.
We are still and always becoming,
strengthened by your presence.
Thank God for you!

Affirmation of Baptism and Naming Ceremony

Welcome in the name of God,
who creates, saves, and calls us
with grace that lasts forever.
Amen.

We are dreamed and formed by a God
who is not qualified by our language or limitations,
who has declared the generous identity: *I am who I am.*

We are claimed and loved by a God
who does not conform, who cannot be contained,
who delights in your holy life and self-expression still unfolding.

We trust that the Holy Spirit has gathered this community
to embody the love, safety, and joy God desires
for your mind, body, and soul—on earth and in heaven.

You are made in God's own image,
worthy of dignity, belonging, and purpose
through Jesus the Christ,
who transforms all things for good.

CELEBRATING BAPTISM

In baptism, you were joined to the death and resurrection of
    Jesus.
Your humanity was claimed in the name of the Triune God,
and the people promised to remind you that
while the world will call you by many names,
your first and forever name is Beloved.

We honor you, Beloved Child of God.

*The person affirming their baptism might share about
the name they have chosen to recognize in this assembly.*

[Name], we affirm your baptismal promises,
your identity as a beloved child of God,
and the Spirit's transformational presence in your life.

[Name], you have been sealed by the Holy Spirit
and marked with the cross of Christ forever.

*A baptismal sponsor or chosen family member
may light the baptismal candle from the Christ candle.*

You are radiant, made in God's own image.
You are the light of the world.
You are a city on a hill, so shine where you are.

God of life, in Jesus you have known the fullness
of our human experience. You were born into human flesh,
into the spectrum of earthly love and fear,
our limitations and longings. Bless [name]
with dignity, belonging, and purpose from heaven.

Pour out your Holy Spirit upon [name];
the spirit of wisdom and understanding,
the spirit of counsel and might,
the spirit of knowledge and the fear of the Lord,
the spirit of joy in your presence. **Amen.**

Affirmation of Baptism or Confirmation of Faith

This worship event offers opportunities for students and members of the faith community to lead. Invite small group leaders, confirmation mentors, godparents, local teachers and coaches, and other trusted adults into this celebration of faith so that many voices are heard and the intersections of faith and life are lifted up. Unless space is an issue, consider celebrating confirmation during a regular worship service to emphasize the role congregations play in supporting the baptized on behalf of the whole church.

This service includes four speaking parts for those affirming their faith. Original faith statements can be added or substituted to fit your community's needs.

Consent: Remember to ask for consent from all participants well in advance of this celebration. Those affirming their baptism should have full agency about public speaking, kneeling, and being touched during the laying on of hands.

CELEBRATING BAPTISM

Welcome in the name of God
who creates, saves, and calls us
with love that lasts forever.
Amen.

Even before you were born and baptized,
God delighted in you and called you Beloved.
You were claimed by the death and resurrection of Jesus Christ
whether you knew it or not, whether you liked it or not.
And the Holy Spirit was equipping you
with unique gifts and talents to share
as a partner in God's creative work in the world.

Lest you grow up thinking that God loves you
from an abstract or accidental distance,
the baptismal promises were spoken to you,
for you, and together with your name.
Your family, sponsors, and congregation gathered
around you in the midst of worship and community
to declare God's love and salvation for you.
This happened on a particular day in human history,
marked by the calendar and the memories
of the people who showed up.
Seeds of faith were planted in your story.
We give thanks for those who pray for you and nourish your spirit.
They are signs of God's promises at work in your life.

You have invited us to gather as witnesses
as you affirm your baptismal promises today.
We celebrate your participation in Christian community,
worship, service, prayer, and study for the sake of
your sacred calling as human beings who are
discovering good purpose and passion in this life.

Voice One: I believe that today is a new beginning, not an ending.
I can affirm my faith as belief that is still becoming,
with wonder, doubts, and more to learn.
Thanks to the layers of promises in baptism,
I get to explore who I am and what I believe
in community with the body of Christ.

Voice Two: I believe that baptismal promises
move and adapt with me throughout my life.
Sometimes they are loud and clear.
Sometimes they are quiet and patient.
There is nothing I can do to break this love,
and it doesn't expire.

Voice Three: I believe in the human tendency
to earn personal success,
to strive for one's own gain,
and the temptation to conquer life alone.
And so the promises of baptism are countercultural.
I will be fooled by the forces that defy God,
but my baptism will continue to tell
God's truth about love, power, and value.

Voice Four: I believe the church makes mistakes
and is far from perfect.
And yet, God does not give up on the church,
but continues to shape ordinary people
for sacred healing and justice in the world.
God is calling us back to who we actually are,
and God can do good in the world through our lives.

Congregation, please rise.
Together with your siblings in Christ,
you wish to profess your faith in God and reject sin.
We make these bold statements
not because we are absolutely certain about these things,
but because we are always becoming faithful to them
and learning to wrestle with these claims
about our relationship with God.
We join our voices with yours
to remind you that we are all in this together.

When you were baptized,
we stood with you to speak God's truth
about power, value, and love.
We promised to reject the voices
that would challenge your first and forever identity
as beloved children of God.

Now we invite you to stand with us
in defiance of the forces of sin and evil,
trusting that the same Spirit who had the power
to raise Jesus Christ from the dead is alive in you.

People of God:
Do you reject the devil and all the forces that defy God,
the powers of this world that rebel against God,
and the ways of sin that pull us away from God?
If so, say, "We do!"
We do!

Do you promise to continue supporting
these children of God,
affirming them through all circumstances
with their first and forever name: Beloved?
Do you promise to hold healthy and safe space for them
to keep growing in faith, so they learn to trust
there is nothing they can do to make God love them
any more or any less than they are already loved in Jesus?
If so, say, "We do!"
We do!

Do you believe in God the Father?
**I believe in God, the Father Almighty,
creator of heaven and earth.**

Do you believe in Jesus Christ, the Son of God?
I believe in Jesus Christ, his only Son our Lord.
He was conceived by the power of the Holy Spirit
and born of the virgin Mary.
He suffered under Pontius Pilate,
was crucified, died, and was buried.
He descended into hell.
On the third day he rose again.
He ascended into heaven,
and is seated at the right hand of the Father.
He will come again to judge the living and the dead.

Do you believe in God the Holy Spirit?
I believe in the Holy Spirit, the holy catholic church,
the communion of saints, the forgiveness of sins,
the resurrection of the body, and the life everlasting.

The assembly is seated.

Your baptism gathered a cloud of witnesses
to speak promises on behalf of the whole Christian church.
Your spiritual family grew
to include sponsors, friends, and church members
who have been keeping those promises
and carrying your faith on your behalf.
Today we ask you to make these same promises,
claiming your call to active participation
in the nurturing of your spirit
and the work of the church on earth.

Will you join us in practicing your faith
and keeping these responsibilities:

to live among God's faithful people,
to pray daily,
to hear the word of God and share the Supper,
to learn the prayers, creeds, and commandments,
to open the holy Scriptures,
to be nurtured by the faith and prayers of others,
so that you learn to trust God,
proclaim Christ through word and deed,
care for others and the world God made,
and work for justice and peace?

Those affirming their baptism: **I will, and I ask God to help me.**

*Those affirming their faith are invited to stand or kneel
in front of the assembly while their family members
and sponsors gather around them.
With consent, they lay hands on those affirming their faith.*

Gracious God,
Thanks to the free gift of eternal life through Jesus,
death's power is destroyed! And, since death isn't so scary anymore,
we are freed for more courage and joy in our daily lives
that can witness to your great love. Continue to bless [name]
with dignity, belonging, and purpose that come from you.
Pour out your Holy Spirit upon [name];
the spirit of wisdom and understanding,
the spirit of counsel and might, the spirit of knowledge
and the fear of the Lord, the spirit of joy in your presence. **Amen.**

Congregation: **We celebrate your faith, your voice,
and your unfolding story as beloved children of God!
On behalf of the whole church on earth,
we will continue to pray for your faith and give thanks for you.
God bless you!**

A Blessing for the Baptized

This is a blessing
that remembers your baptism
and tells the story
even if your memory cannot.

It watched a community
gather around you.
It heard the water poured
and felt the love expand.

This blessing will travel
every distance with assurance
that baptism's promise
does not wear thin over time.

The gift is hardy and sure.
You could not break it if you tried.
Life has a firm grip on you,
Beloved One.

It is more than enough.
And so are you.

SPEAK IT PLAIN

A Swift or Private Baptism

God is present in this thin place,
where heaven's sense of time interrupts,
holding still the hands of our clocks.

Baptism is resistance,
a subversive acknowledgment
that death has a word,
but it does not have the last word.

God is present in this thin place
while heaven's throne room sings
More life and more life still!

Its melody is being written on our hearts.
This is the song until the end of time.
We will sing and believe for each other
until it is the only promise left.

[Name], I baptize you in the name of
the Father, and of the Son, and of the Holy Spirit,
one God and Mother of us all. **Amen.**

God of life and more life still,
Pour out your Holy Spirit upon [*name*],
the spirit of wisdom and understanding,
the spirit of counsel and might,
the spirit of knowledge and the fear of the Lord,
the spirit of joy in your presence. **Amen.**

[Name], beloved child of God,
you have been sealed by the Holy Spirit
and marked with the cross of Christ forever.

Go with Christ, who is the way from death to life. **Amen.**

5

Teaching Liturgy in Worship

"Why don't you just say it like that in worship? If you said it like that, then more people would pay attention and realize it's for everybody."

Thank God for the students who speak it plain. They don't pretend to be interested in long prayers or hide their yawns during worship. What you see is what you get! When we return the favor with unpretentious language and room for interpretation, we are teaching liturgy that invites a fresh curiosity and engagement from the people.

This section includes some ways we can mark milestones, keep baptismal promises, and learn together as an intergenerational community. Inviting young people to lead helps the other generations to perk up and pay attention. Student participation will inspire younger children. Their straightforward explanations and leadership will remind their elders that rising generations do not need to grow up before they have voice and value. They have what it takes to shape church here and now.

Let's give the history of our worship style and theology a fighting chance to be interesting. It never hurts to give a little background about an element in worship, especially since an increasing number of worship participants don't have a liturgical background—or do, but their faith leaders never explained how it became a tradition or defined the very churchy words we use. What traditions and worship components need to be revealed again so everyone can participate more fully?

Celebrating First Communion

Whether your congregation welcomes kids to the sacrament as part of an age-level curriculum or when the child and family decide they're ready, remember that the table is a place where people of all ages need to experience God's *yes*. The world has thousands of ways of telling kids they are too young and not ready quite yet. The church forgets that God chooses simple, ordinary elements such as water, bread, and wine to prevent barriers between promise and people. As worship leaders, we have an opportunity to speak it plain: This is the body and blood of Jesus for you. Full stop.

When children are receiving their First Communion, consider the different ways they might wish to participate and receive attention. Invite families to invite godparents and extended family or serve treats after the service. Would they like their names in the bulletin announcements or on the worship screen? Ask whether they'd like to bring the bread and wine forward with the offering or come up front to help during the Great Thanksgiving, or whether they want to speak part of the liturgy into the microphone. If they prefer less public attention, would they like to help design the bulletin cover, bake the bread, bring Communion to a homebound member after the service? Finding ways to include their variety of gifts reinforces that there are a lot of right ways to celebrate an open table and wide welcome at Holy Communion.

Words for The Meal

Holy God, you make plenty for everyone, everywhere. But ever since the first human beings were created, we've had a hard time trusting this good news. Some do not have enough, while others steal and hoard and use more than is needed.

This meal helps us remember you are generous. And you made us to be generous. And together, all the people who receive Holy Communion make a big, generous body. This mass movement to your table is re-membering your body, putting us back together like puzzle pieces. This taste and sip of heaven interrupts our fear of scarcity with your promise to provide enough for all of creation and satisfy our whole lives.

You are manna from heaven,
> **you are the bread of life.**

You are the widow's jar of flour,
> **you do not run out.**

You are baskets of loaves and fish,
> **the feast that feeds thousands.**

You are a deep well at midday,
> **the living water.**

You are the Lamb of God,
> **you pour yourself out for all people.**

We celebrate with these children receiving their First Communion today. May God give them joyful hearts, open hands, and the courage to come to the table as their actual selves. We believe that Jesus is fully present in this meal—over, under, around, through the bread and wine—so that we can't receive it without getting the gifts of Jesus, too. The logistics are a mystery and God's to tend. We simply trust that where Jesus shows up, there is forgiveness, salvation, and new life that come from heaven.

Insert the Words of Institution and the Lord's Prayer.

The Post-Communion Prayer

Bread of life, you have filled us with love and life we cannot earn. Make us signs of your peace and abundance on earth, for we are the body of Christ, and the world is hungry for the wholeness and life we have in Jesus. Amen.

Teaching the Lord's Prayer

This teaching liturgy invites elementary school students into speaking roles. Equip students with the script well in advance of the worship service so they can practice with a family member at home and with a microphone in the worship space. If children's education has a learning component about the Lord's Prayer, invite all the students and family members involved in that process to the front of the worship space for the Lord's Prayer. Their presence is a visual reminder of the promise we make in the baptism liturgy "to teach them the Lord's Prayer." If your students learned hand motions or American Sign Language to help them remember the Lord's Prayer, they can show the assembly. If they made artwork for each petition, it can be displayed during the prayer.

Introductory Reading

Voice One: The first disciples spent a lot of time with Jesus. They traveled, ate meals, and served together. When they were confused about Scripture, heaven, or God's love, they could just ask him.

Voice Two: Jesus knew the disciples had questions about how to pray. Should prayers be long and use fancy words? Should they be about the things we want or the people who bug us? What does God want to hear about?

Voice One: Jesus told them that praying is spending time with God. Sometimes you talk and sometimes you listen. Sometimes you're alone and sometimes you're part of a bigger crowd. You don't have to have the right words because God already knows your heart.

Voice Two: The disciples still looked confused, so Jesus gave them a prayer to use whenever they didn't know where to start. We still use it when we feel stumped because it's filled with good stuff about who God is and how God loves to take good care of us.

Voice One: So we say it when we're alone and when we're all together. And we say it now before Holy Communion to remind ourselves that, thanks to Jesus, we know God and we have what we need.

Voice Two: So let's pray together the prayer our Lord Jesus taught us . . .

Pray together the Lord's Prayer.

Closing Prayer

Listening God, we are grateful for your desire to be near us. You promise to hear our cries, to receive our thanks, to delight in our joy. When there are no words, your Spirit translates our sighs. When we do not know where to begin, we turn to the prayer that Jesus taught us. Write this prayer on the hearts of these students, so that they learn to trust your glory, provision, and love now and always. Amen.

Children Receiving Study Bibles

The preacher may invite the students and their families forward before the readings and sermon, or perhaps when all the children are invited forward in the service so younger kids can participate. This script can be spoken by the preacher or divided into parts to include family members, children's ministry staff, and Sunday school teachers. Consider asking one of the students receiving a Bible to be the lector during this service.

Script for Presentation of Bibles

A long time ago, it was hard to make books. There were only a few copies of books because you couldn't type the words on a computer and print them out of a machine. Scribes had to use ink and parchment to handwrite every single word, so it took a really long time.

The church didn't have a lot of Bibles. There were enough for the priests and bishops and super-fancy church people who could read in Hebrew, Greek, or Latin, but most Christians couldn't read any language.

Now, if you're the only one who can read the Bible and everyone else has to listen to what you say, that's a lot of power. You could tell people anything you want! You could leave out the parts you didn't understand. You could say all kinds of stuff about God and Jesus . . . and they wouldn't know what's true!

About five hundred years ago, a fancy church guy named Martin Luther started to write the Bible down in German, a language the people in his country could understand. Then he made a bunch of copies with a brand-new machine that made books faster. He started handing them out, and pretty soon lots of people had Bibles they could read themselves.

People brought their questions to the fancy church leaders:

- Did Jonah *really* get swallowed up by a big fish, or was that pretend?
- Why did God let all those terrible things happen to Job?
- You never told us about this grace! I thought I had to earn God's love!

Do you ever have friends or siblings play with your toys and together you make a much bigger mess than you do when you're playing alone?

Well, the same thing happened in the church. The fancy church people liked to keep the Bible and all the questions about the Bible neat and organized for just a few people to use. But thanks to Martin Luther and many other Reformers, there were Bibles and questions everywhere! They got curious and creative, and it made a great big mess because, all of a sudden, everyone was allowed to play.

- Do you think God likes it when everyone gets to participate?
- Do you think God is glad that the Bible is in lots of languages so people all over the world can read it?
- Do you think God's okay with this kind of mess?

Yeah, me too. I think it's the best kind of mess.

So here's the thing. We need your help

- to make the church messy;
- to make sure kids know they can participate;
- to remember how important it is to learn about God together, from each other, at home, and not just at church.

So today your family and the church are keeping a promise we made on the day you were baptized. We promised we would put a Bible in your hands. We promised we would make sure you could read the Bible yourself, so you can get curious about God and Scripture, too.

Careful. It's going to be messy. Some of these stories are confusing, gross, scary, silly, and really cool. This Bible has familiar stories and many you've never heard before. You can read it yourself, out loud, or ask a friend or family member to read it to you.

Because, thank goodness, these days the Bible is for everyone!

Students, these Bibles are study Bibles. We want you to open it up during confirmation at church, but also at home. You can mark it up by drawing pictures or writing notes in the margins. If you wear it out, we'll give you another one.

> Psalm 199 says, "God, your Word is a lamp on my feet and a light for my path."
>
> In Isaiah 55, God says, "The Word that goes out from my mouth does not return to me empty, but accomplishes the thing I sent it to do."

The Gospel of John speaks about Jesus as the Word: "The Word became flesh and dwelled among us, and we have seen his glory."

Family members, we invite you to place these Bibles in your children's hands and say, "Be curious and open to the word of God."

People of God, let's bless these students and their families.

The preacher invites the congregation to extend their hands toward the families as a sign of blessing.

Closing Prayer

Living God, we give you thanks for the many ways your Word invites us into a relationship with you and with each other. Bless these families with curious hearts and open minds, that the Bible would spark questions that lead to more questions, faith that grows and gets messy, and a deeper love for you, through Jesus Christ, the Word made flesh. Amen.

Teaching the Nicene Creed

The Nicene Creed might be the part of liturgy I explain most often. To guests, it might sound exclusive or like belief means certainty. The things we list are not necessarily the most interesting things about the Christian faith in the twenty-first century. Worship aims to invite people into a living story through Scripture, song, prayer, and sacraments. The Nicene Creed can sound like an argument well past its expiration date! Still, we promise to teach the creeds in baptism, and it does reveal a timeless challenge for the church: We spend a lot of time self-describing by what we are not, reacting to external assumptions, and dividing the church with accusations. It's entirely different to come together for a clear and passionate articulation of who we are and what matters most.

This script is similar to the resource for teaching the Lord's Prayer in that it invites students and their families to lead the congregation in what they've come to understand about the creed in Sunday school. Equip a few students for speaking roles and invite families to join their students while they lead the Creed. Create a public art space in your congregation or community to collect statements and images for a living creed, a place to gather testimony about the Triune God and what feels essential to our faith and mission today. I hope that these words will help the assembly hear the Nicene Creed in its historical context and ask them to wonder: What beliefs is God calling the whole Christian church to confess these days?

A Reading in Two Voices

Voice One: Once upon a time, being Christian was brand new and super confusing.

Voice Two: Even more confusing than it is now.

Voice One: Christian leaders spent a lot of time responding to falsehoods and misunderstandings.

Voice Two: Some of those people didn't mean any harm, they just didn't get it.
Others were trying to get rid of Christians by getting them in trouble with religious leaders and kings.

Voice One: They spent the first few hundred years talking a *lot* about who they were *not*:

Voice Two: We're not cannibals.
We believe in one God, not three different gods.
We read and do some of the same things Jewish people do, but being a Christian is different from being Jewish.

Voice One: Eventually, Christians got tired talking about all the stuff they *didn't* believe and decided to write down the things they *did* believe.

Voice Two: It was hard to agree about what to include and how to word things.

Voice One: Should we say *Creator* or *Maker*? Do we really want to include Pontius Pilate by name? Will using the word *catholic* be confusing in two thousand years?

Voice Two: It took a long time to write since a bunch of people were involved.

Voice One: There were probably a lot of rough drafts, arguments, and compromises.

Voice Two: But finally they had a creed to share, a symbol of what it means to be a Christian and to believe in a Triune God.

Voice One: And many Christian traditions, like ours, still use it in worship today.

Pastor: You'll notice that in the hymnal and in the bulletin, it's always printed in bold. We say it all together because believing all this stuff requires teamwork. It's heavy. It's mysterious. We can't prove most of it. For many, there's a line or two that make the creed a tough pill to swallow. And that's okay. Confessing our faith with the creed doesn't mean we have all of this stuff figured out, or that we're not remotely skeptical. It means this is the stuff that sets our tradition apart. This is the stuff we're willing to wrestle with. This is the stuff we carry together.

So if your voice needs to drop out when we mention the virgin birth or the resurrection of the body, listen to the other voices, the other people carrying that part for you and take heart. It's a good way to remember that our faith thrives in community.

Together with the whole church in Christ Jesus,
we confess our faith using the words of the Nicene Creed:
The assembly joins in confessing the creed with the students.

Blessing Students Beginning Confirmation

Most confirmation programs begin when students are in middle school, a developmental stage that is navigating all kinds of rules and systems about free will and belonging. Begin the journey in worship by remembering baptismal promises, reminding their families that confirmation is not a graduation, and modeling faith exploration as more than an extracurricular activity or syllabus.

Bless them. Speak grace that extends beyond requirements. Make their belonging abundantly clear. Hold space for a future in which some of these students have the free will to not confirm their faith publicly. Give these students the honest impression that they have the authority to shape the confirmation experience with their questions, ideas, and needs along the way.

This blessing includes an opportunity for family members to present their students with a symbol of this new beginning. The gift can be unique to each family or on behalf of the congregation. Ideas include a study Bible, a prayer journal, a cross necklace, or a personal letter that includes detailed memories of their baptism day.

Script for Blessing Students

Today we recognize these students on their journey of faith. Confirmation is a discernment process, which means we will discover faith in God through studying Scripture, worshipping in community, learning about the sacraments, building relationships, serving others, and noticing ways our baptismal promises are at work in our lives. Every student and faith journey is unique, and so we honor the different beliefs, experiences, and learning styles of everyone in this program. And, at the end of this program, we will respect the decision each student makes about whether to affirm their baptism publicly.

Remember that confirmation is not school, nor is affirming their baptism a graduation. Our learning together isn't for the sake of certainty, confidence, or a personal achievement that makes them more acceptable to God. Quite the opposite, actually.

Confirming their faith will mean

- they have laughed at the impossible like Sarah,
- they have wrestled with the unknown like Jacob,
- they have felt both big and small like David,
- they have piped up for justice like Esther,
- they have been stirred by prophetic voices,
- they have prayed with words both ancient and new,
- they have heard their own melody in the Psalms.

Confirming their faith will mean there is more of all of this

- more asking and wondering,
- more remembering and reforming,
- more stumbling and serving,
- more hoping and loving,

because we are always confirming our faith. We are living in the thin spaces between baptism and death, where the cross makes no sense and all the sense at the same time.

Jesus says to those who follow him, "All who want to come with me must say no to themselves, take up their cross, and follow me. All who want to save their lives will lose them. But all who lose their lives because of me will find them" (Luke 9:23; Matthew 16:24).

I ask the people of God in this community: Do you promise to continue praying for these young people as they begin confirmation? Will you hold sacred space for the fullness of their unique questions, identities, and callings as beloved children of God?

If so, answer, "We will!"

We will.

I ask the parents and guardians of these young people, will you continue holding their baptismal promises? Will you nurture and share your own faith so that your children can see the beautiful and messy fullness of who you are still becoming?
If so, answer, "We will!"

We will.

Family members, you are invited to present your student with a symbol of this new chapter in their faith journey. While you do this, declare what was true in their baptism: "You are loved beyond measure and a gift from God."

With your young person's consent, place your hands on their head or in the air over their head to bless them. Let us pray,

Closing Prayer

Gracious God, we are still becoming, still being made new, still listening for a word about who we are meant to be. Continue to speak into our lives, to remind us that we are yours, to reaffirm the promises that give us hope and life. Bless these students with the presence of your Holy Spirit, the Spirit of wisdom and understanding, the

Spirit of counsel and might, the Spirit of knowledge and the fear of the Lord, now and forever. Amen.

The families can remain up front for the Prayers of the People. Consider inviting several students to write or lead the petitions. Families return to their seats during the Passing of the Peace.

6

Litanies for Worship

Our words for worship have the power to convey how God values the fullness of our lives: our callings, our relationships, our work, and our seasons of change. This is one of the reasons I like to give airtime to leadership roles and responsibilities during Sunday morning worship. It's an opportunity for people to make promises to one another, acknowledge the importance of healthy boundaries, and participate in a milestone together as a congregation.

I once served a small congregation that gave an ivy plant wrapped in tin foil to each new member, a scrappy symbol of the congregation's personality, humor, and generosity. A young adult on the edges of the community decided to become a member because she loved that symbol. That litany showed her that life on the vine doesn't need to look tidy or perfectly potted.

In that spirit, I invite you to honor the magnitude of the moment without glorifying it. The manner in which we celebrate people and congregations matters. Naming the experience in worship helps the assembly see that this change is part of its faith story and the wider church (and that life goes on). Using plain-speak language will decode the milestone for visitors and members who might not otherwise have context for why the moment matters.

This section includes resources for installing and sending leaders from a variety of roles, and marking major changes such as the birth, transformation, and death of a congregation. The section "Other Blessings" also is well suited for use in worship.

Farewell to a Lay Staff Member

Your ministry among us
has embodied a [personal descriptions] spirit.
Today we give thanks for the ways
you have kept baptismal promises
for so many people in this congregation:
encouraging imagination,
affirming questions,
inviting prayer,
holding boundaries,
blessing the chaos,
and helping others experience safety, challenge,
and love in the body of Christ.

Prayer

Let us pray. Gracious God, bless your servant [name]. Surround them with our gratitude and love in this season of change, that they would sense your presence and delight in their daily life. Thank you for giving [name] to us to know as a sibling in Christ, a steward of your mysteries, and a worker for peace. We release them from their call to [role and congregation], trusting that you will continue to use them to bless the church and the world through Jesus, who is transformed and transforms us. Amen.

Blessing

Creating God, who makes all things new,
prepare your heart and mind for new beginnings.
Jesus the Christ, whose story makes us whole,
knit your love for this call into the fullness of who you are.
Spirit of Mystery, who comes beside us with power,
guide your discernment and delight
from this day on and forevermore. Amen.

Farewell to a Pastor or Deacon

Your ministry among us
has embodied a [personal descriptions] spirit.
Today we give thanks for the ways
you have honored your ordination vows
and blessed so many people in this congregation:
preaching the gospel,
administering the sacraments,
forgiving sins,
keeping confidence,
affirming questions,
inviting prayer,
holding boundaries,
blessing the chaos,
and helping others experience safety, challenge,
and love in the body of Christ.

Release from Call

We are glad for the relationships you have built in this community;
your [pastoral] leadership in our joys, sorrow, and growth; and
the deep spiritual connections you have to members of this congregation and their families.
But today your role in the lives of these members is changed. You are no longer their [pastor/deacon], which means you must decline the invitation to officiate their baptisms, confirmations, weddings, and funerals. This will allow them to build trust, grow, and grieve with their next [pastor/deacon].
Do you promise to honor this boundary for the sake of the health of this congregation and its leadership?
I do.
Do you receive our grace and release for anything that feels unfinished in your ministry here?
I do.
Do you trust our gratitude as you move forward into a new chapter of life and ministry elsewhere?
I do.

Prayer

Let us pray. Gracious God, bless your servant [name]. Surround them with our gratitude and love in this season of change, that they would sense your presence and delight in their daily life. Thank you for giving [name] to us to know as a sibling in Christ, a steward of your mysteries and a worker for peace. We release them from their call to [role at congregation], trusting that you will continue to use [name] to bless the church and the world through Jesus, who is transformed and transforms us. Amen.

Blessing

Creating God, who makes all things new,
prepare your heart and mind for new beginnings.
Jesus the Christ, whose story makes us whole,
knit your love for this call into the fullness of who you are.
Spirit of Mystery, who comes beside us with power,
guide your discernment and delight
from this day on and forevermore. Amen.

For a Congregation Closing

We always have been a living place,
people made of dust and breath
for the mess of joy and sorrow shared.
We bless this congregation's record books,
signs of our shared milestones and memories
that continue to matter and grace the world.
We always have been a Christ-centered place,
keeping the fullness of Jesus and God's love
in the midst of our mission and ministry.

**We bless the cross, a sign that God knows
the fullness of our human suffering
and has defeated sin and death.**

We always have been a hopeful place.
Like the star that guided nations to Bethlehem,
we shine like Jesus, who is not overcome.

**We bless the candles and their light,
signs of Christ's presence in our worship
and in the nighttime of our lives.**

We always have been a songful place.
God has put words and music in our hearts
that call us beloved children, saved by grace.

**We bless the books that guided our worship,
calling us into the work of the people
and forming our faith over time.**

We always have been a quenched place.
These promises have countered scarcity and death
with abundance and life that do not fail.

**We bless this font and the gatherings around it,
for here you call us Beloved already and always,
sending ripples and currents of grace into creation.**

We always have been a nourished place.
God has satisfied us with a simple and holy meal,
feeding us often with forgiveness and signs of enough.

**We bless this table and its settings,
reminded of all the ways we have known daily bread
and glimpsed the feast that never ends.**

We always have been a curious place,
opening Scripture together in community
and expecting to be changed by the word.
> **We bless this Bible and your word made flesh,**
> **which dwells among us as good news**
> **about your presence and great love for us.**

We always have been a sending place.
This is where good courage has fueled our faith
and service to others beyond these walls.
> **We bless this sacred space that calls us beyond**
> **what is already and known into the wilderness**
> **of what is next and, by your Spirit, still unfolding.**

For a New Congregation

The liberty is loud
in this body forming
and being formed
by dust and breath.

I cannot hear
the pressure of how
we've always done it that way
or the fear of loss just yet.

But there are murmurs
of expectation and longing
that rumble when we show up,
brand new and hungry.

Like an infant,
our stomach is small.
It is mostly the work of watching
and holding while we grow.

It is wonderful to be alive
with love and potential,
a gift lean and joyful
for the world.

May God bless this new body
and all its incarnate,
the wonder of beginning
the becoming together.

For New Members

Will you show up with this community for worship, study, prayer, and service to others?
I will, and I ask God to help me.
Will you practice being curious about Scripture, your neighbor, and God's ongoing creation in daily life?
I will, and I ask God to help me.

Will you share your sense of call and unique talents with a spirit of generosity in the life of this congregation?
I will, and I ask God to help me.

Prayer

Gathering God, you knit your people together in the body of Christ and form congregations to do your good work. Be present in our feasting and praying and our worship and service, so that this community reflects your abundance and desire for the church on earth today and always. Amen.

Pastor: We give thanks for the unique stories and talents you bring to this community. The church is a living organism, and your commitment adds value and energy to who we are as a congregation.

Sponsors: We promise to welcome your faith as it flows through life's joy and challenges. We desire for this church to be a safe place where you can show up as your true self and be received with love and grace.

All: **Faith is a team sport, and we are in this together. In this community, we choose curiosity over certainty, and strive to honor each other's faith expressions and life experiences with respect and love.**

Council Member: We also acknowledge that we will fail you. This congregation will both embrace and resist change. Sometimes we will disagree and make mistakes. So we ask that, on this side of disappointment, you promise to stick around for the healing that surely comes. Because if you go before the listening and the mending, you will miss the holy thing about being the church: the dying and the rising, the forgiving and the living. Do you desire to become members of this congregation, investing in the future of this shared mission and ministry?

New Members: We choose the fullness of this community!

All: **We welcome you as members of this congregation, inspired and invested in the ministry we all share. You are beloved, and your presence here is a gift! May God bless these new relationships and our common call as agents of God's mercy and the abundance the world needs!**

For Clergy Misconduct

This call has been woven through
more than one story, more than a little life,
braiding together people and promises.

It is both blur and boundary,
the ordained intertwine, always asking
for careful accounting to protect the form.

There was a day when
the weight of these things became real,
fabric yoked, hands blessing what might be.

So much of it has been honored and true,
but some things have been torn apart,
too frayed for repair from the chancel.

Once set apart for hope and healing,
a new call to decrease,
to relinquish this power and space.

There is most certainly mercy,
but it cannot be administered from within
the tangled, wounded erosion of this fault.

This call has been woven through
what already has been, but now
the loom will learn new patterns and shades.

For Congregational Grief and Trauma

Welcome in the name of Jesus,
who knows the fullness of our grief
and bore the weight of our trauma
in his own body on the cross. Amen.

God, our source of hope and strength,
your Holy Spirit has gathered us together
despite our fear and unbelief,
so that isolation does not have the last word today.
Our hearts ache and our bodies weep,
signs of lament and pain we cannot manage alone.

LITANIES FOR WORSHIP

Like the Easter disciples—
weary, overwhelmed, and afraid—we hide behind locked doors
in need of your presence and peace.
Appear in this place with solace and love
that already has known and claimed us,
even and especially in the face of great pain.

Show us your hands and your side.
Let us touch the signs of your life on earth
and your suffering and death among us.
Hear our loud cries sound
over the chasm that divides already
and not yet.

Renew your vows today,
the words that remain steadfast
even and especially in the face of
this world's broken promises
and our own mortality.

Whisper "Peace be with you" and breathe
new life into these dry bones.
Breathe peace while we moan and crack
with the ugly business
of resurrection from the dead, becoming
a spirit of restoration and hope where
there is only a graveyard of despair.

SPEAK IT PLAIN

For Congregations Coming Together

I do not remember Jesus calling us
for competition or comfort set apart,
or describing faith in any certain terms
that reward our isolated maintenance.

But he might recognize this vulnerable hope,
careful discerning that merges dreams,
the stark awareness of our mortality
that defies earthly metrics for holy story.

Everything old will pass away.
Even the large stones will be torn down.
When we are together, it is more gift than threat,
and we are freed from the weary winning
and the sorry sport of saving ourselves.

What courage for systems to die to themselves,
to be buried with dignity and gratitude,
released from storing up treasure right here!
They have lived and trust there is still more.

I do not remember Jesus calling us
to hang onto what we have made,
but he might recognize these hands
holding lightly what is ours to tend for a while.

He might recognize these eulogies
and the grief that still waits for us
in the dying and the rising, in the mess of
becoming together over and over again.

For Installing Lay Leaders

You have been entrusted with rights and responsibilities that affect all of us
and the ministry we hold dear. As leaders of this congregation,
we ask for your commitment to the values and mission we share in Christ:
Do you promise to be faithful to the gospel of Jesus in the governance of this church?
We will, and we ask God to help us.
Will you notice and nurture the gifts, questions, and ideas of the people you represent in this role?
We will, and we ask God to help us.
Will you communicate with proactive and faithful transparency for the sake of the whole organization?
We will, and we ask God to help us.
Will you acknowledge the unknown and unknowable about being church, practicing honesty, humility, and courage in times of change?
We will, and we ask God to help us.

Do you promise to discern and do what is right, even when it disrupts our status quo, and especially when it asks something difficult of us for the sake of our neighbors?
We will, and we ask God to help us.
People of God, do you promise to support our council leaders with your blessing and prayers?
We will, and we ask God to help us.

Prayer

Equipping God, give us new eyes to see your vision and ears to hear your plan for this community of faith. When we lead and serve with confidence in your bold grace, our labor is not in vain. Bless each of these leaders with courage and kindness, patience and tenacity, good humor and great hope, so that together we are able to do immeasurably more than we could have asked for or imagined on our own. Amen.

Blessing

May God fill your hands and heart with work that is real.
We bless your vocations:
your home, your work, your relationships, and all the ways you serve.
May God give you the strength and passion to lead well through thick and thin.
We bless your successes and failures:

all the ways you try, create, and explore in the name of Christ.
May God root you in wisdom and faith and Sabbath rest.
We bless your leadership and your self-care:
May this work refresh and inspire you.

For Interim Leaders

Like Miriam, Aaron, and Moses, you have been called to lead this beloved community through wilderness years. [Description of specific circumstances.]

You are helping us navigate the cultural and spiritual transformation of this community with faithful and generous leadership. We give God thanks for your spirit, for your visions and dreams that help shape our commitment to the gospel in liminal seasons. May the Holy Spirit continue to guide your leadership for the sake of the church and the world.

From the prophet Joel: The Lord God declared, "I promise to dwell in the midst of my people and to wipe away shame. Then I will pour out my spirit on all flesh; your sons and your daughters shall prophesy, your old men shall dream dreams, and your young men shall see visions. On men and women, on the oppressed and free, I will pour out my spirit" (2:28–29, author's translation).

Prayer

Gracious God, in baptism you sealed and marked your servants [names] with your Spirit and the cross of Christ forever. Continue to bless the fullness of their lives with a spirit of wisdom, courage, and grace so that they remain faithful to your will in the midst of uncertainty. Grant this community a tenacious spirit, that we would be alive with the breath of your Spirit and the good news of Jesus today and always. Amen.

For Installing a Pastor or Deacon

Presiding Minister: On behalf of the Christian church and this denomination, it is my duty and joy to install our sibling in Christ, [name], as [deacon/pastor] at [congregation]. I ask leaders from this call process to present the documentation that makes this invitation official.

Congregational Leader: **After prayerful discernment and thorough consideration on behalf of this congregation, we have extended a call to [name] and present them for installation today.**

Presiding Minister: Thank you for sharing your time and energy with this discernment process. It's a blessing to the whole congregation.

[Name], in accepting the call to ministry of word and [service/sacrament], you promised to uphold the holy Scriptures as the word of God, to confess the creeds and the Lutheran confessions as theological context for understanding the word of God, and to preach the gospel of Jesus Christ.

Will you continue to study Scripture, pray for God's people, serve others for the sake of justice, and keep your baptismal promises in this community?

I will, and I ask for God's help.

Will you set an example of healthy leadership, keep the Sabbath, practice boundaries, care for relationships, and seek the resources and support you need to maintain a wholistic well-being?

I will, and I ask for God's help.

Will you bear witness to God's love in the world, helping this congregation build trust, seek justice, and share love with the wider community?

I will, and I ask for God's help.

Will you discern and do what is right, even when it disrupts our status quo, and especially when it asks something difficult of us for the sake of our neighbors?

I will, and I ask for God's help.

May the God who has called you in baptism and set you apart in the ministry of word and [service/sacrament] continue to bless you with the conviction and grace to do these things for the sake of Jesus and this community of faith. Amen.

People of God at [congregation], will you receive [name] as a minister of word and [service/sacrament], a called and ordained leader in the church on earth, a sibling in Christ, a fellow human being who will love you and, occasionally, fail you?

We will.

Will you pray for [name], support and honor their leadership for the sake of the ministry you share, and bear witness to our unity in Christ?

We will.

[Name], the office of [position] is entrusted to you.

With consent from the Pastor or Deacon, the congregation is invited forward for the laying on of hands and a blessing.

Prayer

Empowering God, you share creative power with your people, inviting our participation and leadership so that the kingdom of heaven is revealed in human activity. Bless [name] with wisdom and compassion as [pastor/deacon] at [congregation]. Entrust good and holy things to their care and equip them to lead with faithfulness and courage we know in Jesus Christ. Amen.

7

Special Services

Worship remains the central and primary experience for Christian communities. It's a good barometer for how a congregation wrestles with faith and serves in the world. Whom do we regularly bless by name in our prayers? What adjectives do we employ to describe God? Do we hear permission to show up sad, suffering, and broken in this space? Can the words in worship help people ask new questions, reclaim their true identity, and hear a call to action?

As a worship leader, these services feel like especially thin space. We can't be sure who will show up, or whether we have prepared to offer what they need. But then the Spirit is so clearly present in the wide-open spaces of the sanctuary, filling in gaps between the eleven people who needed a word in the midst of grief or addiction that cold winter night. The Spirit is so clearly there when the space is packed with people representing a constellation of belief systems, gathered in one place against all odds, because it's time to marry or bury their loved one. The Spirit is so clearly there when hospitality and worship leaders honor the personal space and boundaries of others, modeling consent with everyone they serve.

Special services can draw newcomers into the liturgy who are less familiar with our worship style, Scripture, and theology. We can adapt to welcome guests into the experience with inclusive language. It can teach in the midst of ritual. It can ask questions and bear promises the world does not offer. So why would we want to bury all that treasure under four-syllable words only our ancestors and insiders can understand?

For Trauma-Informed Worship: Some Guidelines

Creating a trauma-informed worship experience requires additional training for worship leaders and hospitality volunteers. Here are some practices that can help people who have experienced trauma feel safe and welcome in worship.

Prepare the Space

1. Prepare ushers and greeters to think about safety differently. Survivors of trauma might require extra personal space or be uncomfortable participating in portions of the service that expect physical touch or movement during the service. If the layout allows, make a small room nearby available as an alternative space. Candles, icons, chairs, and Bibles can help people feel

connected to the service even if they need to step away from the assembly.
2. Before the liturgy begins, worship leaders should make it clear that participation is not mandatory. Every instruction about standing, singing, or moving within the space is an invitation, not a command. We're glad they've come. And if they need to leave before the service ends, that's okay too.

Put It in Writing

1. If lighting is adjusted during the service, consider printing the lighting cue in the bulletin or on the screen, so the assembly can anticipate that change to the environment. Sudden or loud noises should be avoided or explained ahead of time. If the service involves an element that invites physical participation, include detailed instructions that reinforce this element is elective, not expected.
2. If Holy Communion, laying on of hands, and prayer stations can be located in a variety of places throughout the worship space, this helps participants engage a location that is most comfortable for them. (For example, I might be willing to visit a prayer station located behind most of the parishioners, but not up front in the chancel or stage area.) Be very specific about what participants can expect from an experience that invites movement. The explicit language can build trust and reduce anxiety. Here are two examples:

> *We celebrate an open table at Holy Communion. That means everyone is welcome to participate in the meal.*

Ushers invite people to come forward by row beginning in the front of the assembly. At the railing you can stand or kneel as you feel comfortable. The bread is homemade, and if you need a gluten-free wafer instead, just ask the server. The chalice has two chambers. The bigger one contains wine, and the smaller one contains white grape juice. At this service, we dip the bread or wafer into the chalice before consuming it. If you forget and eat the bread or wafer first, don't worry. God is abundant, and we'll get you another piece. You are also welcome to come forward to receive a blessing instead of communion or to remain in your seat. Please let an usher know if you'd like to be served where you are, and we can come to you.

Prayer stations are located throughout the sanctuary. If you decide to visit a prayer station, the ministers of presence are ready to listen, pray, lay hands on you, or anoint your forehead, but will not make assumptions or touch you physically without your consent. You may also ask them to wrap your shoulders in a prayer shawl that is then yours to keep.

Make Resources Available

When training worship leaders and hospitality volunteers, invite them to add a few key phone numbers to the "Favorites" list in their cell phones. These resources should be introduced with education about why and when to call each organization for assistance, and how to seek a worship participant's consent before employing them. With regular training, your team can have a synchronized approach to caring for church as a safe space for trauma survivors. Numbers might include:

- National Suicide Prevention Hotline
- RAINN (Rape, Abuse, Incest National Network) Hotline
- Your local police precinct
- Your county's adult mental health crisis and child crisis hotline
- Other local advocacy, protection, support, and legal-aid agencies, including food shelves, free meal locations, and so forth.

Note: Also consider having these numbers on a handout in your brochure racks or other readily accessible places for worshippers to pick up and take with them.

Practice Consent in Worship

What does it look like to practice physical consent at church? Church staff and volunteers can model healthy boundaries and respect for the space of others, proactively transforming church culture and equipping people with healthy practices for daily life. Here are a few guidelines:

1. Before touching a child to bless them during Communion, ask to put your hand on their head or shoulder. If their behavior is reserved or shy, just speak to them or offer a high five. They do not owe an adult physical contact or pleasing behavior.

2. When greeting visitors or sharing the peace of God, do not assume it is okay to hug someone simply because you are a person who likes to give hugs. Make sure that physical touch is mutual, and that the person who holds less social power feels respected by the exchange.
3. Just because a form of physical touch was accepted once doesn't mean it becomes a requirement. Church should be a place we can come even (and especially) when we don't feel like sharing our physical space or giving and receiving physical touch.
4. Special services (foot washing, imposition of ashes, anointing) that include an opportunity for physical touch should include explicit instructions about the participants' options. For example, teach the assembly in advance how to communicate that they prefer oil or ashes on their hand instead of their forehead.
5. If hosting a station for laying on of hands or blessing, ask the participant how you can support them and offer a few examples verbally. It might sound like overcommunicating, but Christianity has good theology for the sacredness of our human bodies. Consent is respectful stewardship of each other's physical beings as service to Christ.
6. Be careful about requiring certain behaviors or interests before accepting others into a common belonging. This is often meant with humor, but having to prove you belong in a Christian community by liking coffee black, trying a cultural food, or adopting a particular posture during worship can be experienced as exclusive or forced assimilation.

SPECIAL SERVICES

For Blessing a Neighborhood

The congregation may choose to visit each stop together as a group, or the prayers can be printed on separate cards with locations and handed out after worship so people scatter from worship into all corners of their community for simultaneous prayer. Additional petitions may be added.

For Bus Stops, Train Stations, or Airports

We pray for our neighbors who wait for public transportation, who commute for work or school, who rush from one place to another. We give thanks for the healthy motion of pedestrians and bicyclists, the labor of public safety workers and builders, and the access public transit provides for the most vulnerable among us. Keep people safe and alert in their comings and goings, so that we see and honor one another, even if only in passing.

For Libraries, Community Centers, Public Parks, and Health Clubs

We pray for public places that encourage well-being, social connections, and lifelong learning. Bless the employees with curiosity and compassion. Abide with those who show up yearning for safe relationships, a break from responsibility, or a chance to feel useful. Use these gatherings to teach the church something new and important about hospitality and wellness, so that we become centers for spiritual health and wholeness in you.

For Restaurants, Grocers, Bodegas, and Corner Stores

We pray for those who grow and harvest food, care for the earth, ensure products are safe, and transport goods, and the stores that make food accessible here in this neighborhood. We pray for those who require assistance to afford food, those who lack time or skill to make healthy meals, and those who struggle in their emotional relationship with food. Bless these shop owners, their workers, and all who purchase goods. Bless those who slow down to eat with deep appreciation for the plated miracle. Remind us that your provision is more than enough and of our call to share generously with one another.

For Government and Social Service Agencies, Schools, and Day Care Centers

We pray for the helpers, the teachers, the caregivers, and the tenderhearted professionals who dedicate their labor to the vulnerable among us. May these be safe places where trust and hope can flourish in the lives of those whom they serve. Grant these organizations the funding and community support they need to bless our neighbors with the wisdom, dignity, and joy they need to thrive in this life.

For Affordable Housing

We pray for safe housing, just landlords, and affordable rent in this neighborhood. We confess the ways housing policies have been created and protected to segregate people and diminish the life of some. In Jesus, you have shown us that loving our neighbor transforms communities and means saying, "Yes! Right here in my backyard." Make us instruments of heaven's hospitality right here, a witness to the abundance and belonging you desire for all of us.

For Hospitals, Clinics, and Counseling Centers

We pray for those who tend to our physical and mental health, those who seek healing for patients and clients, and those who practice medicine with courage and kindness. God, you know the despair and fear we carry in our bodies and minds, our mortal weakness and the suffering we feel. Abide in the listening and waiting, the treatments and tests. Give comfort and strength to all who long for newness of life.

For City Hall and Police and Fire Stations

We pray for public servants, for those who vow to serve and protect the public. Bless these leaders with wisdom and courage to do justice for the little, the last, and the lowly; to embody your Spirit with a nonanxious presence; to listen and honor all people with dignity; and to work for peace that asks something of those so often in control. Dismantle systems rigged to help only some, to protect those already powerful, and to conceal what needs to be revealed. Grant safety to those who sacrifice their own for the sake of their neighbors in need.

For the Watershed or Nature Preserve

We pray for the rivers and streams, the running water that gives life to this land and connects us to the whole of creation. We repent for the ways we have stolen and abused the land, commodifying what is source and gift meant to flourish beyond our instantaneous greed. We have drawn arbitrary lines all over this land with borders and roads, but the watershed does not comply with our maps, and the animals roam where they will. Bless the wild beasts and the water that flows all on its own. Make us mindful of its freedom and beauty in our midst.

For Corners, Margins, and under the Overpass

We pray for our neighbors who sleep outside, whose possessions pack down into a pillow at night, who manage each day without an address or enough eye contact to feel human. We ask for God's love and protection among sex workers, people who live with mental illness, those caught in the cycle of addiction, and youth rejected by their families because of their sexual identity. Transform our hesitation and pity into justice and mercy for those who live on the margins of our consciousness. Give us ears to hear their stories and eyes to see them with the love of Christ.

For Local Businesses

We pray for the local economy and for workers and their wages. Teach us to invest in each other and to be thoughtful about what we consume each day. May these businesses reflect the values of this community and the people they serve, building trustworthy relationships with the whole supply chain and deepening our appreciation and awareness for the labor that helps us thrive.

For Houses of Worship

We pray for faith leaders and the places our neighbors gather for worship. Hear the prayers raised by people in every tradition, and make us defenders of the freedom we all have to worship safely. Banish the fear and hate from our hearts so that we live together in peace as neighbors united by a spiritual call to goodness on earth. Give us a holy curiosity and respect for one another, trusting that we are all created in your divine image and have much to learn from one another.

For Healing and Wholeness

Gathering Words

We feel anxious.
> **So we gather.**

We feel pain.
> **So we gather.**

We feel sorrow.
> **So we gather.**

We feel lonely.
> **So we gather.**

We feel weary.
> **So we gather.**

We feel fractured.
> **So we gather.**

Silence for reflection.

Breathing Together

We begin with our breath,
thanking our bodies for bringing us here,
for guiding us into community,
for this presence in the body of Christ.

The leader helps the assembly take three deep breaths together and then invites them to be seated.

Prayer

Living God, it has taken everything we have to gather.
And, now that we are here, we trust you to keep your promise,
to dwell in our midst with love that mends our wounds.
Tend to the fullness of our lives with the compassion of Jesus,
who knows the human struggle like us,
who has suffered and mourned with us,
who has carried the weight of sin for us.

Send your Spirit to guard this space from our pride and nerves.
Declare it safe shelter for our actual selves,
where performance and shame are released
because you already know and love us completely
and you delight in our true nature unhidden. **Amen.**

Confession and Forgiveness

When we confess, we acknowledge the ways
we have been living apart from relationship
with God and each other.

**We confess our sin, our separation, and our suffering.
Grant us mercy, undeserved and extravagant,
so we are restored to dignity, belonging, and purpose
that come from you.**

We are loved by a God who keeps promises,
whose grace is restless to find and free us,
who calls us beloved from the first day until the last,
always eager to welcome us home.

Friends in Christ, your sins are forgiven.
May your liberation be a gift
to the world still aching for freedom.

The assembly is invited to come forward to receive the laying on of hands. Songs and hymns about healing and restoration may be shared at this time.

Laying On of Hands

[Name], you are known and loved by the God who made you,
by the One who accompanies your joy and sorrow
with the promise of life after death.
May you be strengthened by the love of this community
and the healing power of the Holy Spirit, now and forever. **Amen.**

Prayer

God, you are the source of all healing.
Thank you for coming near
the broken and despairing parts of life,
even seeking them out.
And though we have felt lost and forsaken,
we remember the cross and trust that your loving presence
knows every inch of our human story.
Send us with your Spirit for company,
like wind that whispers tender and fierce love
into our courage and hope each day. **Amen.**

Blessing

May the weary weight you have carried here
surrender to the power of connection and communion.

May the fullness of your actual self find warmth and recognition
in the presence of Jesus, the risen One.

May the healing presence of God flow through you,
soothing the cracks of your soul, anointing your whole life. **Amen.**

SPECIAL SERVICES

For Recovery and Mental Health

Suggestions for preparing the space and worship elements:

If this is a small assembly, consider organizing the space so the assembly is seated in a circle or a U-shape. The altar table should be placed so it is approachable for the assembly.

Place a basket of stones near the entrance to the worship space and invite participants to choose a stone before gathering. This stone represents the heavy things they carry with them into worship. Place a basket on the altar to receive stones during the service.

If serving Holy Communion, consider serving grape juice exclusively at this service.

The Serenity Prayer and the Prayer of Good Courage are well suited to this service and can be read together as an assembly.

During the offering, invite people to write a prayer request or word of gratitude down on a piece of paper and place it in the offering plate. Explain that later in the service these will be redistributed so that we each will read someone else's aloud in prayer.

The Twelve Steps can be read as an assembly, or each person can choose a step for personal meditation during the service. The musician can curate a contemplative arrangement while people pray and reflect about one particular step speaking into their life. When it's time to read the Twelve

Steps, people read only the step they were using aloud, listening to others read the rest.

Prayer petitions might include these topics: stigma, shame, resources, policy, safety, treatment, access, family, friends, sponsors, sobriety anniversaries, milestones, suicide awareness, abuse, neglect, professional and personal caregivers, and underrepresented communities.

If the service does not include Holy Communion, you might include the opportunity for people to be anointed with oil on their foreheads or hands. They can come forward for the anointing and a few words of blessing based on the readings or theme. Or you can invite them to turn toward a neighbor and bless one another with the sign of the cross.

Gathering Words

The stone you chose represents the heavy things you carry into worship. It's a physical reminder that you can bring the overwhelming and weary things here. If at any point in the service you wish to be free of it, there is a basket on the altar to receive it. You are also welcome to keep it or bring it back another time.

This worship service is filled with invitations, not requirements. Please participate as you feel comfortable and trust that this assembly will respect how you decide to be present in this space.

Confession and Forgiveness

We bless the name of God,
who seeks out the lost,
who names us beloved,
who restores us with great love.
Amen.

Faithful God,
> **We are here to admit our brokenness and fear.**
> **We get rattled and lose track of what's true.**
> **We focus on the imperfections of others.**
> **We pledge our allegiance to unworthy things.**
> **We have failed to embody your goodness.**
> **Forgive us, God. Be merciful.**

In this is love, not that we loved God but that God loved us and set Jesus to bridge the gap and extend a word of forgiveness beyond all of our shame and sin. Everything we hide and hate is God's to destroy through Jesus. We are free, and now we are called to live and love like we are free. Breathe a sigh of relief and joy, friends. God is already revealing heaven in your newness of life.
> **Alleluia! Amen.**

Holy Communion

Jesus sat down to dinner with his disciples for the last time, breaking bread and drinking from the cup in communion with one another and with God. Jesus knew that Judas would betray him later that evening and that Peter would deny knowing him after that.

Still, he invited them to the table and called them by name. He loved them and knew that God needed to experience suffering and dying in order to destroy the hold it has on us and to restore the fullness of God's life and love in creation. So Jesus took the bread in his hands and blessed it. He broke it and gave it to his friends, saying, "This is my body, given for you. Do this to remember me." And then after supper he took the cup of wine and said, "This is my blood, poured out for you and for all people to forgive sins. Do this to remember me."

It is the greatest gift, this table where Jesus is both the host and the feast. In word and action, Jesus declares that God is all in on restoring us to new life. Now there is nothing—absolutely nothing!—that can separate us from God because Jesus has accomplished everything we cannot.

It's hard to know how to receive this gift, the God who knows rock bottom and perfect love in Jesus. So we respond simply and together. We pray using the words Jesus taught us, and then we hold out our empty hands.

The Lord's Prayer

Distribution of the Elements

Blessing

May God bless your body, mind, and spirit
with the grace to trust you are enough,
and you are made new each day in Christ.
    Amen.

For Separation or Divorce

Gathering Words

When people asked Jesus about divorce, he spoke to the complexity of unbecoming a committed couple. He described the messy and intimate way marriage tangles lives together and the impossible task of separating what has been shared.

We gather to recognize that what has been in marriage cannot be undone or forgotten. This relationship was an important part of your life for a time and will continue to shape the uniqueness of both of your futures.

When you married, there were witnesses there to affirm and bless the vows you made to each other. Today we gather to offer our witness to your decision to [separate/divorce], to be signs of God's love and our love for you in this season of grief and change.

Release from Promises

I, [name], release you, [name], from the promises you made to me as your spouse and to our marriage.

Those recognizing their relationship may wish to name memories or experiences for which they are grateful. They also may exchange new promises about how they plan to navigate financial and legal arrangements; social boundaries; or sharing custody of children, pets, or property.

Poem (Based on Psalm 6)

There is isolation
in the rage of things that fall apart,
the unraveling that lingers too long
and wears me out with grief ever new.

I hear their whispers,
the ones who once stood with promises,
who feasted at our table with joy.
They loiter, and it is agony.

I ask for God to return to me,
to restore the parts of me that atrophy, and
to dry these endless tears
so I might see beyond the pain.

Transformation will not be swift,
nor elegant and easy,
but God has heard my cries,
and that is not nothing.

And I will wait, while this shame is removed,
to carve out space between
what has been and what can still become,
my face turned to the east and expectant.

Prayer

Creative God, you have a reputation for making new things out of chaos, brokenness, and even death. Reshape this ending, so it is also a new beginning that reveals more life, more light, and more wholeness for your people through the love of Jesus.
Amen.

Blessing

May God bless you with patience for the time healing requires,
compassion for yourself and for each other,
and the courage to come home to who you already and always are:
God's own beloved.
Amen.

For Celebration of Marriage

Greeting

On behalf of [couple], welcome to their celebration of marriage.
We have been gathered by the Spirit of God to bear witness
to their love and the promises they will make to each other.
We stand as evidence of the wide community surrounding [couple]
with prayer, support, and mutual joy.

Declaration of Intention

The following is asked and responded to by each marriage candidate. Ask ahead of time which pronoun each one in the couple prefers you use (him, her, them, they)

[Name], will you have [name] to be your [spouse/partner], to live out the promises of marriage? Will you love, comfort, honor, and keep [him/her/them] and, in all seasons of joy and sorrow, be a faithful partner to [him/her/them] as long as you both live? If so, say, "I will."
I will.

Community, your presence today speaks volumes, a manifold witness to surround this couple and the vows they will exchange. Do you give your wholehearted support and care to their new life together? If so, say, "We will."
We will.

Prayer of the Day

God of love and life, we have known mercy and faithfulness by your example to humankind and in your relationship with the church on earth. Pour out your blessings on [couple], that they may nurture their marriage with gifts of compassion, strength, and faith that come from you, through Jesus, who is your love made flesh, and the Holy Spirit, who dwells with us now.
Amen.

Readings

Reflection

The officiant should keep in mind that no one came to hear their sermon today and efforts to be funny are usually and notably not. Commentary meant to prove how well you know one or the other person, gender stereotypes, and remarks about their fertility and family planning are unsolicited and awkward. Keep it short and sweet. Bless them with the good news that marriage is really hard work, but they don't have to do it all by themselves. This community and God will be there to cheer them on as unique people and together as a couple.

Marriage Vows

Marriage vows can be traditional or original compositions, but should clearly express a commitment to love and faithfulness until death parts the couple. Consider using the same set of vows so that the promises being exchanged are mutual and do not demand more or different expectations of faithfulness from one partner than the other.

Blessing and Exchanging Rings

Generous God, we give you thanks for your example of unconditional love and faithfulness to your people. Like the rainbow you set above Noah and his family and the starry cosmos above Abraham and Sarah, may these rings be signs of the faithful covenant [couple] have made with each other. Amen.

Each person in the couple repeats the following in presenting a ring to the other.

[Name], I give you this ring as a sign of my love and faithfulness.

Acclamation

[Couple] have promised their commitment to marriage in the presence of God and this community. We rejoice in their vows and celebrate their new life together as [spouses/partners].

The assembly may applaud since the couple is now officially married. Other symbols of marriage may be given or music shared at this time.

Marriage Blessing

Gracious God, pour out your blessings on [couple] and on this first day of their married life. Nourish their promises with gifts of your Spirit, and strengthen their relationship with support from loved ones. Guide their life together so that they are never far from your promises, which bear witness to love beyond measure through Jesus Christ. Amen.

Prayers of Intercession

We pray for [names] as individuals, for who their actual selves already and always are loved and claimed by God in Jesus. May they build trust and hope with each other, so they are filled with good courage for every season of life together.

We pray for this new marriage and for committed relationships everywhere. May they be honored and celebrated as signs of God's grace.

We pray for this assembly gathered today and for all families and communities. May they be safe and loving places for people to grow in faith and life together.

We pray for those who feel grief, pain, or sadness today. May there be patience and compassion between people, healing in our tears, and comfort for all who mourn.

We pray for our ancestors and descendants, our place within the order of things, wisdom that surrounds us, and holy wonder to send us into each new day.

We offer these and all our prayers to God's gracious care, trusting that we are fully known and loved through Jesus, who experienced the fullness of life and death among us, who knows our joy and suffering, who goes ahead to prepare a place for us in heaven. Amen.

The Lord's Prayer

Blessing

May you remember today for the promises you made to each other.
May you remember today for this wide village of love and support.
May you remember today for the God who delights in your life,
    this and every day. Amen.

Introduction of Couple

It is my honor and joy to present for the very first time [couple and new relationship].

Recessional

Postlude

For a Memorial Service

Gathering

We gather today to hear the good news of Jesus and to remember [name]. We give thanks for the gift of knowing them in this life, pray for their homecoming in heaven, and offer each other love and comfort in the midst of our grief.

Thanksgiving for Baptism

We begin by giving thanks for baptism. God uses ordinary water and a sacred promise to turn our human story into a "Yes, and . . .". Yes, we are mortal. We make mistakes and eventually die. And we are so fiercely loved by a God who calls us precious, forgiven, and worthy despite every effort to define human value according to earthly measures. This grace is thanks to Jesus, who came to earth to accomplish everything we cannot, who gives us everything we need to be our real selves, together with God.

Creating God, you made heaven and earth. You formed us from the dust of the earth and called us very good. Your breath gave us life.
We glorify your creation.

Saving God, you were born to live with and like us. You have felt our suffering and joy so that we are never alone. You died so that we, too, can live a new and eternal life.
We praise your salvation.

Sustaining God, you stir up our faith and comfort our sorrow. You gather your church for the sake of hope that carries us forward one day at a time.
We worship your abiding presence.

To you, O God, be glory and honor forever.
Amen.

God of Life, your Holy Spirit has gathered us together to remember [name]. Be present in our sorrow with holy compassion and good care that help us mourn. Give us faith to trust that death does not have the last word, and help us hang on to the hope we have in Jesus, who is resurrection and life for all people.
Amen.

The service continues with readings, words of remembrance, and the resurrection promise proclaimed.

Prayers of Intercession

Gracious God, you gather your people together for grief and gratitude. Help us hold space for every emotion in these first days of memory and mourning. Abide in our faith, our hope, our doubts, and our fears with strength and peace that come from heaven.

We pray for your whole church across time and space, for faith communities of every tradition and nation. Help us reveal your goodness and mercy in this life, so all of creation is blessed by the good news of Jesus.

We pray for those who feel the weight of [name]'s death deeply today, for those tending to the logistics of death, for those remembering other loved ones who have gone before us. Come beside your people and their sorrow with love that is patient and kind, with peace that comforts and mends.

We pray for those who feel distant from your care, those who doubt their sacred worth, and those who ache because their pain is too great to bear alone. Send your Holy Spirit to illumine our paths with your light so that we remember we belong to each other for the sake of your glory.

We pray for wonder in the midst of things we cannot understand. Open our hearts and minds to the mystery of salvation, the sacrifice of your love, the forgiveness of our sins, and the resurrection to life everlasting.

We bless you, God, for your servant [name]. Their life revealed your image and brought light to the lives of many. We have seen in their friendship your compassion, in their weakness your strength, in their humility your glory, in their integrity your goodness, in their faithfulness glimpses of your eternal love.

Strengthen our faith so that we, too, may trust that nothing can separate us from your love in Christ Jesus, that your life is now [name]'s and will one day be ours.
Amen.

Commendation

Merciful God, we entrust [name] to your eternal care. Look upon them with favor and joy, as a child of your own creation, a sheep from your own fold, a sinner you redeemed with love on the cross. Receive them into your holy presence, into your everlasting peace, into the light and song of all your saints.
Amen.

We go forth with audacious grief, but keep living with hope that comes from Christ.
Amen.

For a Graveside Committal

This service may be used by a church leader but is written especially for family members to use if they do not have a church leader present to officiate. A committal service is brief and does not usually include music.

If the event includes a military presentation, that should occur prior to these words of committal and the promise of life everlasting.

Welcome

We are gathered to hear the good news of Jesus Christ and to remember [name]. We give thanks for their life on earth, pray for their homecoming in heaven, and offer each other love and comfort in the midst of our grief.

Prayer

God of Life, we are made in your image and hardwired to seek meaning, relationships, and connection. In Jesus, you experienced the fullness of humanity and felt the weight of every love and loss in this world. Be close to us now as we mourn the loss of life and remember our own mortality. Give us faith to trust that death has a word, but not the last word. Help us hang on to the hope we have in Jesus, that there is life after death and love that endures forever. Amen.

Scripture Readings (Psalm 23 or Psalm 46)

Poem: "A Blessing for This Earth"

This is the place.
It is both goodbye and homecoming
for mortals born of stardust
and breath from heaven.
The stillness is
both foreign and familiar.

SPECIAL SERVICES

This is the place
we will come to remember,
we will mean to visit more often.
It will cause us to wonder
about the sounds and smells
beneath our feet.

This is the place
that writes the death of our person
into the history of this world
with specific coordinates,
even more accurate as time melts
boundaries between creature and creation.

This is the place
reserved to honor a life that still lives
in us, blowing like windy
memories from our mouths
just often enough to help
our unbelief to glimpse death rising.

If there is a floral arrangement, the leader might invite family members to take a flower at this time. Small handfuls of sand may also be used to cover the casket or urn if it is being placed into the ground. If this graveside committal is in place of a memorial service, consider adding words to commend their spirit into God's care here.

Committal

We, the living, are still novices to death and remain perplexed by the mystery of human bodies committed to the earth and human spirits commended to heaven. We, the living, do not pretend to understand the resurrection of the dead, but we lean into these promises anyway.

Merciful God, we trust that you have always loved [name] and are with them even now. We commit [name] to the earth. Like the first human beings in the garden, you formed [name] by the dust of the earth and gave them the breath of life, declaring them "very good." We return [name] to the ground knowing that you have made life from ash and dust before, that death is not the end, and that you keep your promises for the sake of life, love, and light that cannot be overcome. Amen.

The family might recite the Lord's Prayer or a psalm together at this time.

Blessing

May God's blessings and comfort continue to find us,
even and especially in the logistics of death,
the enormity of our loss,
and these first seasons that will feel so different
without [name] living among us.

Go in peace. Christ is with you.
  Amen.

Acknowledgments

I am published thanks to my supportive editor, Scott Tunseth, and the keen-eyed editorial review of Carol Throntveit. Thank you for embracing this project and encouraging my voice.

I am grateful for the leaders who have asked me to write something fresh and accessible for their special occasions, trusting my theology and language with an important moment in the life of their community. It always gives me great joy to write something and then notice how it sounds and feels while it's being unleashed in a faithful context.

I am shaped by the congregations I've served and the worship experiences we've shared. You welcomed many pieces from this resource while they were still literary and liturgical experiments. Your curiosity and faith are profound gifts.

I am a better pastor thanks to my friends who do not attend worship or consider themselves religious. Our conversations about God and spirituality inform the way I try to welcome, teach, bless, and hold space for a variety of people and questions that the church has not given worthy consideration.

ACKNOWLEDGMENTS

I am surrounded by colleagues and mentors in ministry who are gifted writers and bivocational mavericks. I am shaped by reading what they write and a proximity to their passion for language and the people God loves.

I am challenged with good questions about worship and church by my three children, who shape my words, perspective, and sense of God in our midst.

I am in love with my husband, Matt. He didn't know what he signed up for when he married a liturgical nerd, but no one wrangles three small children in worship quite like him. I am grateful for his endless affection for all of who I am.

Purchasers of this book have permission to make copies of portions of the book intended for group use and response. Access this downloadable content by searching for "Speak It Plain" at fortresspress.com. Open the pages by entering the following code: CARLSON2020.

About the Author

Meta Herrick Carlson (she/her/hers) is a pastor and writer living in Minneapolis, Minnesota. She serves a two-campus congregation that used to be two totally separate churches with different histories and styles. This ministry is challenging and exciting because they are all learning how to let go and lean in for the sake of a shared future. Meta is passionate about cultivating leadership, healthy systems, and preaching that moves us toward mercy and justice.

Meta's first book was *Ordinary Blessings: Prayers, Poems, and Meditations for Everyday Life* (Fortress Press, Spring 2020).

She married a person named Matt who fixes things she breaks and waters all the plants. Their three kids are loud, sticky, and fiercely loved.